What She Said What I Heard

How One Man Shut Up and Started Listening

STUART WATSON

SPARK Publications
Charlotte, North Carolina

What She Said & What I Heard:
How One Man Shut Up and Started Listening
Stuart Watson

Designed, produced, and published by SPARK Publications
SPARKpublications.com
Charlotte, North Carolina

Cover photo courtesy of Michael LoBiondo

Softcover, October 2020, ISBN: 978-1-943070-98-5
E-book, October 2020, ISBN: 978-1-953555-00-7
Library of Congress Control Number: 2020917848

For Lorraine,
a universe of one

Our family: (clockwise from lower left) Colleen, (my wife) Lorraine, Erin, Glynis, me, and Jack. Mint Street. Charlotte, NC. Summer 2005. Courtesy Michael Harrison Photography.

TABLE OF CONTENTS

. . . .

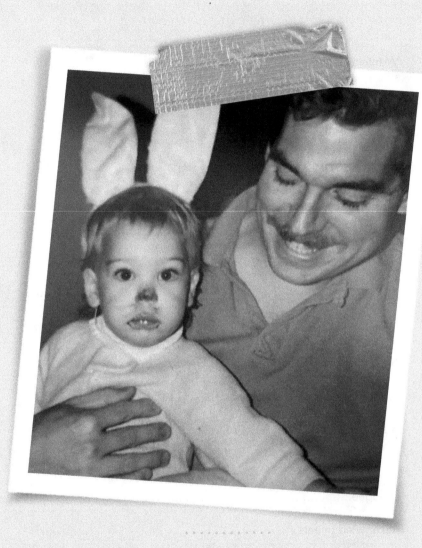

Me with my oldest daughter, Erin.
Halloween, 1986. Toledo, Ohio.

AUTHOR'S NOTE

. . . .

I confess. The only way I got these stories down was to trick myself. I gave my inner critic the month off. Told him this was all just content marketing for my podcast or a speaking gig. No biggie. With less at stake, the guy stopped interrupting long enough for me to tell it. I struggled for years to write a memoir; all I got was a rambling mess, 406 pages, and a hefty bill from FedEx Kinko's. But once I told myself I wasn't Proust or Mary Karr or David Carr, it all lined up. It helped when I began calling my writing "personal journalism."

"Get the chron!" the newspaper editor said, back when they were a thing. The chron? The chronology. Some call it "the tick-tock." What was the time stamp on the security cam? When was the victim last seen? When was the perp at the ATM? What came in between?

Journalism's five W's provided answers for intimate colloquy.

- "Who?" supplied strong female protagonists: birth mother, adoptive mom, sisters biological and adopted, one wife, and three daughters. (To be clear, I always call my birth mother "mother," and my adopted mom "mom," ditto for father/dad).

- "What?" offered inciting incident, action, even dialogue. She gave birth. They took me away. She asked herself, "What kind of a girl gives away her baby?"
- "Where?" contributed the setting: the Georgia State Lunatic, Idiot, and Epileptic Asylum, Crown Hill Cemetery, the frat house soaked in sour beer.
- "When?" sorted the mess into some order, columns in a spreadsheet.
- "Why?" summed it up to a fine point. Here's my takeaway: let go. Let go of being right. The moral of my story: there's hope. It'll get better. We heal.

Hearing my pitch, a published author told me, "That's not content marketing. It's memoir."

"OK," I said. "Whatever gets it done." It's my story. You can just as easily verify the basics, or debunk certain details changed to protect the innocent or made up by my fallible memory. The journalist in me tried to get the details right, but I'm sure it won't be perfect.

I made one big mistake on the front end. I kept saying it was all about the women. It's not all about the women. It's all about me. I can't speak for the women. It could be I got them all wrong, but I tried my best to do right by them. In the end, I figure if I get me right and give thanks for their presence, I'll do right by them, too.

"You do realize it's a trope," my youngest daughter said. "Women who exist just to teach men a lesson." She said they have fully formed lives quite independent of mine and deserve their own books. This is true. They're not bit players. They do not exist merely in relation. They are each entitled to volumes of their own. I just can't write them. I can't dictate their story for them.

Having my mom, dad, and my full-blood sister die, I see I have limited time and more limited options—just three by my count:
1. Tell my own story.
2. Leave it for someone else to get wrong.
3. Be good with my story never getting told.

"Cain't nobody tell your story but you," said my friend Yolanda. It hit me like a bolt. She was talking to a roomful of people. I'm the only one who wrote it down.

After the Yolanda revelation, I went to too many funerals, read too many formulaic obits, heard too many vague eulogies. Soon enough, too soon, any day now, they'll be talking that shit over my dead body. I'm gonna beat 'em to the punch. Supply my own material for the memorial.

I may not get it totally right. But they don't know. I lived it. Cain't nobody tell it but me.

My youngest daughter, Colleen, reading
at Limekiln Lake, Adirondack Mountains,
New York.

PREFACE

. . . .

"Stop talking. You're wrong."
Therapist's name withheld at her request.
Charlotte, North Carolina
2018

On Listening

After I made a crude comment, a woman at work slapped me hard across the face. In the midst of my ranting, my therapist cut me off: "Stop talking. You're wrong." My wife told me point blank: "Sweetheart, you are not an empathic listener."

Three women over the span of thirty years taught me important lessons. The only question is whether I would learn or keep doing the same stupid man stuff, insisting I was right.

Frequently wrong, but never in doubt, my male ego wants to do three things:
1. Look good.
2. Be right.
3. Keep control.

The closer I get to the truth of how my ego acts, I:
1. Look bad.
2. Am wrong.
3. Lose control.

As long as I keep talking over these women, I learn nothing. As long as I dig in, double down, and defend the indefensible, I get nowhere. Whenever I am closed off or shut down, I stay stuck. If I'm arguing, I'm losing. The behavior is its own punishment.

Depending on how far I am willing to go, I could end up all alone, my willful ignorance imposing its own suffering—solitary confinement brought on entirely by self. I imprison me. I could lose the respect of my daughters because of some careless comment. I could be cut off from my wife because I refuse to acknowledge my part in turning a simple disagreement into a heated argument. My colleagues could turn their backs because I don't take their complaints about my boorish behavior seriously.

The past few years in our culture have brought with them a long litany of men whose fundamental contempt for girls and women is made plain. I don't know anything about those men. I have a full plate answering for my own words and deeds. I offer no excuses, only lessons, the occasional hard-won insight.

I'd much rather write a book, produce a podcast, and make films and speeches about how I got the money, the girl, and the CEO gig. I'd love to write only about success (#winning). This is mostly a different story—the recitation of ugly failures. Sorry. It seems to be the only way I learn.

Truth be told, I only had money because I was blessed with generous parents who adopted me. I never "got the girl." I married a strong woman. I fell totally in love with her through wild fate. We're still married decades later because we work really hard at it. At work, I've never made it to a C-level suite. On the contrary, I was told to clean out my little cubicle one Friday and not to come back. I sued them. We settled. I'll never go back.

This is the great gift of my experience: if I become willing to look bad, be wrong, and let go of the need to control my story, huge lessons await me.

My peaceful life on the other side of those lessons is its own reward.

My birth mother, Helen Brett, as a nursing
student at Georgia Baptist Hospital School
of Nursing. Atlanta, Georgia. Late 1950s.

MAKING MY MOTHER CRY

. . . .

"What kind of a girl gives away her baby?"

Helen Brett Schmid
Birth mother
Emanuel County, Georgia
Summer 1958 (recounted 2015)

On Shame

She was standing in her kitchen with a tissue. We'd taken a break from filming her interview when she said it. I'd made my mother cry.

"What kind of a girl gives away her baby?"

That baby was me.

I felt kinda shitty that I'd made an old woman cry ... and frustrated that it wasn't on camera. Because I'm a monster, OK?

It was 1958 when she got pregnant with me. Her father and the Baptist preacher did what men did back then. They shamed her. And then they cooked up a scheme for her to get rid of it. Me. It. Whatever.

That scheme involved shunning this poor woman (a hopelessly naive twenty-two-year-old, no longer a girl and barely a woman).

The two men sent her to a boarding house in Macon, Georgia. There, she would tend to old folks to earn her keep. She'd stay out of sight while she got big enough to call attention to herself. At nursing school, they said she was at home. At home, they said she was away at school. Nobody compared stories.

Turned out, that scheme was quite the rage at the time. It was called adoption. The Georgia Department of Public Welfare was in on the deal. I've got the paperwork. I started life as a little white welfare baby, a ward of the state sent to a foster home with a passel of other kids. Some magazine writer hung a name on this era. Called it "The Baby Scoop."

I have struggled to come up with my own words for what happened to mother and child. I have settled on the word "amputation." The mother grows old toting the phantom body of an infant in her gut. And the child grows up with the invisible scar from learning that its mother loved it so much that she cut it off and gave it away.

But that's all my stuff. We're told Mother Mary kept all these things in her heart. My mother shoved the shame way deep down, where she'd never have to think about it. And it stuck. Buddy, you won't believe how it stuck. When I contacted her forty-five years later, let's just say I was a mixed blessing.

"What kind of a girl gives away her baby?" Well, white girls mainly during this era. It was just economics, the law of supply and demand. Black families kept the children of single mothers tucked away within the family, with Gramma or Auntie. Infertile couples wanted children that looked like them—hair, skin tone, shape, the whole bit. They did not want children who did not look like them. This was true of couples of any race. But many white couples had the money to buy Barbie and Ken.

When the boys came home from war, some of them couldn't conceive. Their mothers and wives in their new cracker-box houses kept asking about kids. Meanwhile across the country, some other clueless couple was fogging up windows. America had not yet begun to look to places like Korea, Romania, Guatemala, and Sudan for a UN family.

The age of first "consent" had dropped. And so did a million or so babies. I'm one in a million. Thus the institution of adoption changed. I can't say it "was born." It's more like this big church-and-state backed adoption scheme was … adopted.

My mother's lifelong shame was not really about me at all. It wasn't about being caught having sex outside marriage, or even the stigma of "illegitimacy." (I was a little bastard long before I became a big one.) No, my mother's shame was that she disappointed her father. My mother loved me enough to tell me her truth. She was the Good Girl, the firstborn of six, the favorite, who fell from grace. She fell hard.

When her father found out about her pregnancy, his blood pressure spiked so high, he was almost hospitalized. As we say in the South, "He near 'bout had a stroke." He was trapped between impossible choices that he made for her: keeping the child and enduring unending shame, or losing his firstborn grandchild. He picked the latter. She went along.

Lintorn Anthony Brett was a self-made farmer who pulled cypress from the Georgia swamps, stumps from the fields, and crops from the land. He took the whole family to a little white church in the country every time the doors opened. Family dinner, church, holiday gatherings—all Bretts were present and accounted for. This was non-negotiable. Nobody took a pass and sulked in their room. He'd whip your ass.

To hear my mother and her family tell it, family meant the world to "Dada" Brett. But "faith" came even before family and farming. So he arranged for her to give me up.

My maternal grandfather drove to Macon and picked up his daughter the day after I was born. She was alone. He met her in front of the hospital and helped her into the truck. Then he said words she'd never forget: "I guess I'll never meet my oldest grandson." He never did.

When she sheds tears now, it's not for her, nor for me. I'll just tell you what she said: "Broke his heart."

WATCH, LISTEN, AND LEARN
To hear Helen tell her own story, visit ManListening.com to view a video.

"

The mother grows old toting the phantom body of an infant in her gut. And the child grows up with the invisible scar from learning that its mother loved it so much that she cut it off and gave it away."

. . . .

My birth mother, me, and my full-blood
sister, Esther Schmid Bristow. Boston,
Massachusetts. November 2007.

GIVING BIRTH

. . . .

"Oh, honey, you don't have the power."

Helen Brett Schmid
Birth mother
Macon, Georgia
April 8, 1959 (recounted 2004)

On Forgiveness

My birth mother gave me up for adoption on the day I was born. She never held me, or nursed me, or laid me on her heart. The nurses weren't supposed to tell her my sex. One of them slipped up and said something to the effect of, "No wonder she was in labor so long; he's such a big boy." That nurse was reprimanded.

Of course, I always wondered what happened to my mother, how exactly I came about, who my people were. I really kind of gave up hope of ever knowing.

But then I became an investigative reporter by trade and had four kids of my own. I survived trying to slowly kill myself with vodka, which is possible, but I do not recommend it—takes way too long.

Once I sobered up for a decade, I wrote to the state of Georgia to formally ask for what is called "non-identifying information." That means some poor social worker (a woman, of course) had to paw through a bunch of secret records and type up a fuzzy report about the circumstances of my conception, delivery, and handover to the state. No names. No places. Nothing to allow a snoopy reporter to put two and two together and come knocking. God no.

This particular social worker slipped up like the delivery nurse. She typed eight single-spaced pages. Plus, she sent a few documents with names and locations mostly covered up. Mostly. It was enough.

I put two and two together and found my mother.

I wrote her a letter in my own block scribble. It began, "Dear Helen."

She wrote me back in some sappy greeting card. Said I should call. There was too much to write.

I was a forty-five-year-old man when I first met my mother. We settled on Augusta Regional Airport as the setting for our first face-to-face meeting, not because either of us flew, but because it was a convenient landmark between me in the big city of Charlotte, North Carolina, and her, in tiny Kite, Georgia. I drove my canary-yellow MINI Cooper with a black roof. She drove an old, white Dodge Caravan.

There were no cameras present to record the event, no background music, no slo-mo buildup. But the friendship that began that day with swapping photos and stories in an airport lobby is a singular highlight on the game film of my life. It began the healing of generations of wounds.

We went to lunch at a nice place in an old house in North Augusta, across the Savannah River. I said something I had always wanted to say.

"I forgive you," I said.

She just laughed.

"Oh, honey," she said. "You don't have the power to do that."

I imagined myself the hero of my own story, the brave investigative reporter who solves the mystery of his own identity, finding his mother after all those years, and promptly proceeding to heal lifetimes of shame with three words. With no shortage of hubris, I conceived of little ole me as the originator of forgiveness, the healer, the master, the fixer.

My mother did what mothers do. She put me in my place. She taught a middle-aged son an unexpected lesson. Alone in a hostile universe, humans lack the capacity to forgive. I can't form even one side of that equation. I can't offer forgiveness, let alone heal her heart.

I did not conceive me—not as superhero and not as wailing child. She and my father, a drunk like me, conceived me. And even then, weren't they just the blind agents of some nebulous purpose, of a power beyond our ability to understand?

I cannot conceive of the shame of the single, young Southern woman who missed her period in the hot summer of 1958, the pure terror of that. No man knows the trouble she's seen. Women do. My father was not in heaven. My father was on the next plane smokin' out of Atlanta.

That woman lost her firstborn, brought to term and handed over sight unseen. Then she lost her husband to vodka and the invisible wounds of war, a casualty after the fact. Then as an old woman, just last year, she found her only daughter, my sister, dead on her bedspread.

At this point I could understand it if my mother lacked all faith in a benevolent universe. In my book, she gets a pass. Go directly to heaven, old woman. You have suffered enough.

Yet somehow, she still has faith. I'm not sure I do. But I think she's been forgiven, and I didn't do it.

"

*Weren't they just the blind
agents of some nebulous
purpose, of a power beyond
our ability to understand?"*

. . . .

Unidentified maid holding me.
Albany, Georgia. August 1959.

BATMAN, JESUS, AND LOUISE DUKES

. . . .

Name unknown
Babysitter
Albany, Georgia
August 1959 (recounted 2020)

On Grace

Weed was never much my thing. I just loved to drink. But one day freshman year, I did a bunch of bong hits, got pretty baked, and saw a vision. It was a group of three round-faced Black women, looking down at me as though I were an infant, their hair wrapped tightly near the scalp and backlit by a bright light, so I couldn't quite make out their faces.

In my mental state, I took this to mean my mother was Black. And to my mind, Black means many things, and they're all interesting. So I was kinda excited at the prospect of being biracial. Or maybe I was just looking for a way to erase white guilt.

Ever what it was, when my DNA results came back, imagine my disappointment at being the whitest man in America. We're talking mayo and marshmallow on white bread. We're talking Casper the

Friendly Ghost white. We're talking Pat Boone, minus "Speedy Gonzales." Not Aryan so much as pasty Anglo. BO-RING!

Then one day I found this black-and-white snapshot of a Black woman in a white maid's dress. She's sitting in a chair I recognize from our living room in my parents' home at 1226 Hilltop Drive in Albany, Georgia. (Pronounced awl-BEN-ee, not like the capital of New York.) She is alone—no other round-faced women in the picture. Her hair is not wrapped. And there is no bright light. The back of the photo is dated August 1959, the same month a welfare department social worker in Macon handed me over to my mom and dad. I was four months old, fat, and fresh out of foster care.

I've asked around a little bit among Mom's living friends to see who this caregiver was. No answers so far. I promise you that I'm not done looking. The novel coronavirus COVID-19 stalks Albany, Georgia, as I write, but as soon as the coast is clear, I'll resume pursuing leads on the ground.

Unlike my best friend's mom, Kathryn Stephenson (aka Snooky Butt), and her other contemporaries, my mom couldn't seem to settle on one maid/babysitter for much longer than a few years. There was Louise Dukes, who got her nursing license and moved to Washington, DC, where I heard her son Tony became a cop. There was Cilla Mae, who dipped fingers full of Rainbow Sweet Snuff inside her lip and hit the back screen door to spit a long brown stream into the boxwood, scattering the cats sleeping in the pine straw beneath. And I remember Robbie, who pretended to discipline us by chasing my sister and me around the house with a leather belt, all of us laughing so hard we bent double.

Among her prized photos and letters, my mom intentionally left us a pair of typewritten instructions to sitters for our care. In one letter, Mom addressed our overnight sitter, who was white. In another she spoke to Ms. Dukes, the daytime maid and childcare provider, who was Black. My mom and dad were taking a rare and exotic long weekend jaunt to Bermuda. In the note were times, dates, menus, recipes, locations, worst-case scenarios, and lists of phone numbers for every imagined emergency. Depending on your disposition, you could see the notes as obsessive or endearing.

A whole universe exists in that pair of documents. It is a cultural artifact articulating a world long gone, where one woman addresses another woman and then a third, speaking volumes about race and social strata and relationship. It's really a whole 'nother long story.

My wife, Lorraine, and I took a number of long weekends to New York in the twenty years or so we had small kids at home. Other than a few phone numbers, I don't think either of us left so much as a thank-you note, let alone typewritten pages with the home telephone number for a pediatrician.

Two things struck me from Mom's notes. One, she said I could stay up past 8:00 p.m. to watch *Batman*. (YESSSS!) Two, Mom instructed the nighttime sitter to "hear the children's prayers." So all jacked up on caped crusader, I kneeled at my bedside and mumbled, "Now I lay me down to sleep, pray the Lord my soul to keep …" as someone kept watch. First Batman, then Jesus, then finally, babysitter.

Lost in all this: who were these caregivers, these Black women holding little white children, mothering them? Didn't they have kids of their own? What happened to their own kids? What did their kids have for dinner? Who cooked for them? Were they watching Batman? Saying their prayers alone? Who heard them? And how did these women regard this pudgy little white boy eating second helpings of spaghetti with the sauce from his mom's recipe—the one with the ground beef from the A&P? Was I just a paltry side hustle for these women? Or did they develop a genuine affection for me? What do I owe them? How do I ever thank them? Repay them for their many kindnesses?

Had they chopped me into tiny bits and made rich, red spaghetti sauce out of my fatty flesh, placing me in Tupperware in the freezer, you would probably know their names. But they didn't, of course. So I have snatches of memories, uniformly warm, some jumbled and fuzzy from too many hits on the old bong.

I read somewhere of a study about regular interaction with people we might dismiss as bit players in our lives: the dry cleaner, the waitress, the receptionist. The study found that when these people go away, replaced by "the new girl" or the new machine, we take an outsized hit of loneliness and disconnection. Whether we wish to acknowledge it or not, we rely on these daily doses of basic human decency.

Nowadays there is such a thing as using one's voice for a straight up transaction, such as compelling a machine to play a song or flip a switch. And then there are human relationships, which involve flesh and blood. True—many a human relationship is defined by money or class or caste, circumscribed by the false and fleeting values of this world. But they are nonetheless human.

And finally there is the singular story of transaction and relationship between white men and Black women in the American South, a tortured history unique in the millennia of homo sapiens. I have no answers for that, only questions. At the time of this story, I was a fat little boy living in a white bubble. I don't know if Jesus heard me say grace over a plate of mom's spaghetti. But I'm grateful Louise Dukes did.

"

*What do I owe them? How do
I ever thank them? Repay them
for their many kindnesses?"*

. . . .

Mom holding me. Albany, Georgia.
Fall 1959.

THE BRIDGE CLUB

. . . .

"Now you will listen ...."

Nell Martin Watson
Mom
Albany, Georgia
1960 (recounted 2015)

On Infertility

Nell Kerns Martin Watson told stories. She and her people came
from Lee County, Georgia. The only reason you might know Lee
County these days is by the famous people from there—Major
League Baseball's Buster Posey of the San Francisco Giants or
American Idol breakout Phillip Phillips or country pop star Luke
Bryan. But if you come from Leesburg, Georgia, and you have four
names, then you have four layers of stories, each layer blending
into another woven back and forth with rich, warm, distinct flavors
playing off one another. That's my mom.

Mom taught me to tell stories. I listened to learn. I absorbed her
soft endings to words sounding like "ambrosia"—camellia, Eufaula,
sustah (for sister). I told a story at her funeral. It starts with a fact,
adds a bunch of stuff I made up, and ends by revealing the truth of

our relationship. And because I'm the only living soul who knows what parts are true, I get to make my own history.

Mom took me by herself to drop me off at college, in my case Vanderbilt University, in Nashville. Dad had come with us for visits. So had my sister Liz, who followed two years later. You can tell this is the true part because Liz is still around to contradict me if it's not. Pesky things, witnesses.

Mom was driving the family car, a Chrysler (pronounced KREYE-sluh). We went to a real Nashville diner called Mac's Country Cookin' before it was torn down to make way for a shiny place called Caviar & Bananas. This I could not make up. *Sigh.*

She parked on the oval outside Kissam Quadrangle (now leveled and rebuilt) and across from the clock tower at Kirkland Hall (still standing) and the statue of the Commodore—Cornelius Vanderbilt. She turned to me from the driver's seat. I felt awkward. Sure, we'd see each other again, but it would never be the same.

"Goodbye, son," she said. "I know you'll do good."

"Well," I said.

There was a beat.

"Well what?" she asked.

"It's 'well,' Mom. 'I know you'll do *well.*' The adverb, not the adjective."

As I recall, she told me I would "do well" to get out of her car. So of course I became an English major.

Before embracing my destiny as a grammar snob, I first shopped multiple majors. I dropped out. I drove a Yellow Cab. I flunked out. I stocked the bar at the Exit/In, the listening room once featured in Robert Altman's film *Nashville.* I drank quarts of malt liquor in brown paper bags, all while sitting on a wall beside

Baptist Memorial Hospital. I waited tables at the Red Lobster up the street from WKRN-TV. I bussed tables at a revolving restaurant on top of a hotel overlooking the limestone-columned Capitol. I only went back to school and finished because Lorraine wouldn't marry me unless I did.

"You're so close," she said. "If you don't finish, you'll always regret it."

So I did for her what I would not do for my mom. I finished. I got a bachelor's degree from Vandy. And Mom developed a newfound respect for Lorraine, in spite of her being a Yankee, worse yet, a New York Yankee.

Lorraine did one more thing that made my mom forget all about that Yankee stuff. She got pregnant. She made my mom a gramma. And Mom was ecstatic! Over the moon.

My mom and dad had never been able to get pregnant. For Lorraine and me, it wasn't a problem. We ultimately cranked out four kids. My family planning was a two-drink minimum. So I never understood why not being able to conceive a child was such a big deal to my mom, not until years after she died. I went to visit an old friend of hers, a war bride from England named Betty McKemie.

Mrs. McKemie played bridge with Mom and the rest of the ladies around folding tables for fifty years, through kids and grandkids and losing kids. This same group of women played cards through Kennedy, Vietnam, and the NASA moon shot. Their friendships survived when some didn't think the country would. They'd migrate from home to home in their dresses with their cigarettes and their lipstick and their covered dishes for lunch, this week's hostess making a sinful dessert that everyone ate. It looked like a scene from *The Help* only a lot less bitchy.

Everyone at those bridge tables except my mom got pregnant and had kids, some more than one, before Mom and Dad finally adopted me. So one day after Mom died, I invited myself into Mrs. McKemie's home in Avondale Estates near Atlanta. She fed me cheddar cheese straws, soup, and salad she'd made herself. She asked me to join her for her afternoon swim. I declined—too worried she'd make me look bad even though she was in her nineties. And she told me stories I'd never heard before and helped me see my mom in a new way.

Betty had tales of German bombs dropped in her front yard, unexploded, her brothers nearly killed, and having to call the British ministry of whatever to come defuse the damn things and haul them off. So I guess infertility was the least of her worries.

Betty told me one day Mom was chatting away about me and what cute little thing I had done this time—pulled my toes or sucked my hand or some other act of genius. And some of the women at the table moved on in the conversation, less riveted by my hand sucking, I guess. And Betty said Mom brought card play to a stop. "I listened to *allll* of your stories," she said to her friends. "Now you will listen to one of mine." You go, Mom.

Compared to a lot of the bridge club and the net income of the "Greatest Generation," I guess I've never done very well. But Mom always believed I'd do good.

WATCH, LISTEN, AND LEARN

To hear Nell Martin Watson tell her own story, visit ManListening.com to view a video.

"

I never understood why not being able to conceive a child was such a big deal to my mom, not until years after she died."

. . . .

Me and my youngest daughter, Colleen,
enjoying the earth and sky. Grand Canyon
National Park. Arizona. July 2018.

THE PLANE-EATING PINE TREE

"You'll get your piece of the sky someday."
Blonde girl draped around boyfriend
Crown Hill Cemetery
Albany, Georgia
Early 1970s

On Hope

I grew up in white suburbia across the street from a cemetery. So when mom told us to go out and play, we had two choices: the swamp behind our house or the open field with the occasional headstone in front. Often as not, we picked the graves.

A teenager we called Brockie Brock once coached an entire sandlot baseball team in what is now the somber-paved approach to the praying hands and little angels of Crown Hill Cemetery. Those were the days when it was owned by the Pate family, long before big corporations began vertically integrating graveyards with funeral homes and I dunno—hospitals?—and creating Big Death, the death industrial complex.

The Pate boys sold ten-foot cedars cut from the back side of the cemetery as Christmas trees. When we were small, there was a preschool—a glorified daycare—smack-dab in the middle of the cemetery. Growing up, death and life were not cut off from one another.

We kids flew kites in the cemetery. Our beagles occasionally strayed there off leash. We played hide-and-seek behind the bigger mausoleums in the middle. The older kids smoked weed there, perhaps contemplating mortality or decrepitude. If you wanted an ICEE (not a Slushee) to turn your tongue blue and freeze your brain on a broiling south Georgia day, you took the shortcut through the graves to get from our street to Taylors Market. To us, Crown Hill was less a place of mourning than an amusement park where we'd include the dead in our games.

We were respectful. We didn't walk on graves. We didn't graffiti the granite. We'd pack it in when Kimbrell-Stern Funeral Directors put up the green tent and covered chairs at the side of a crisp, freshly dug hole, red clay piled discreetly to the side. We were gone long before the black limos and the hearse pulled up. No one in a suit had to shush us or shoo us away.

So it made perfect sense that I would take my new prize toy airplane to fly it around the open cemetery. I'm sure I asked for this plane because I saw it on TV. I'm thinking now that it was Mattel's SuperStar Sky Show that you now occasionally see on eBay. It had a captivating commercial with an earworm of a song—something about getting your piece of the sky. The plane had a battery-powered motor and interchangeable discs in its belly—not electronic, but real rotating discs with zigs and zags that prescribed the flight plan. The plane would turn in and out, banking like a race car on a road course. I was completely infatuated. I held in my hands a portal to my piece of the sky, my own private corner of azure.

I stuck that damn thing in the top of a pine tree. First thing. Couldn't have rescued my piece of the sky with a hook-and-ladder team. It was crushed. I was crushed. My one chance at the sky, forever lost. I crumpled to the ground crying.

A skinny, blonde girl draped around her boyfriend walked past. Oh yeah, some people dated and probably did other things in the cemetery, things that were way beyond my experience. It was possible in this place to be conceived and buried within walking distance of the same spot. Talk about your cradle to grave.

"What's wrong, kid?" she said to me. I explained that all my hopes and dreams had just been dashed by a plane-eating pine tree.

"It's OK," she said to me, her boyfriend tugging her away. "You'll get your piece of the sky someday."

It was a fragment of poetry, this message from a passing stranger. Was this skinny girl actually an angel? I would believe it. Like many Americans, I believe in angels. I just don't believe they look anything like the sweet cherubs on top of babies' graves. Safe to say, of all the things women have ever said to me, this one stuck for some reason. It stemmed the tears of a boy and opened a tiny ray of hope.

My parents' ashes are buried in Crown Hill now, just off one of the northeasterly points of the crown, at about two o'clock. If you look it up on Google Maps, you may see more octagon than crown, eight wedges stemming from a circular hub in the middle, dotted with mausoleums. No kite flying. No sandlot baseball. No Christmas trees.

Even so, I still sometimes visit when I'm in town. I drive up. I don't play. At least not there.

Right now, I am playing with words. My mom gave me this freedom to play.

She and my dad died the same day in the same room of the same disease. We arranged one funeral, one urn, and one slab. My mom died about twelve hours after my dad. She followed him into the darkness of dementia and into the light of whatever is next. Technically, I inherited my portion of her estate, so she gave me the freedom to sit and type these words to you, while others go out and pull a paycheck.

You don't own sky the way you don't own hope. It wanders over in an unlikely form. And it owns you. And the only way to hang on to it is to share it with someone who is crumpled on the ground.

"

The only way to hang on to hope
is to share it with someone who
is crumpled on the ground."

. . . .

Paula Allen, me, and Beverly McGhee.
Just friends (sigh). Spring Prom.
Albany, Georgia. 1976.
Photo courtesy of Larry Patrick.

THE MEDICAL MISSIONARY

. . . .

She just smiled.

Helen McCorvey
English teacher, Deerfield-Windsor School
Albany, Georgia
1977

On Identity

As a high school senior, I aspired to be Albert Schweitzer, thinker of deep thoughts, healer of bodies, great white hope for darkest Africa. I had never heard the word "paternalism." But I couldn't pull off the brushy mustache. That and I sucked at biology 101. Let's face it. I didn't know myself at all.

Helen McCorvey tried to set me straight in a way so subtle that I missed it the first time. Mrs. McCorvey (a.k.a. Miz Mack) taught me English. She treated students with respect, but she was no pushover, so she made lots of "favorite teacher" lists. She taught *The Little Prince* in high school. And among other things, she taught me reading for hidden meaning, writing for clarity, and reading my writing out loud, which gave me the concept of voice. It was a lot.

Her husband, Paul, was a sports columnist for the *Albany Herald*. He covered the Great Religion of Georgia (and Alabama and Mississippi and Louisiana and Texas)—football. That meant when two drunks would get good and lit up long about 2:00 a.m. on Saturday and start arguing about Herschel Walker's stats, they would call Paul McCorvey AT HOME to settle a bet. He was better than the reference librarian, the Google of football, on call 24/7.

I never played football. I beat three drums at once in the marching band (that shit got heavy). And I argued first affirmative on the debate team. I decorated the gym for the homecoming dance and the Elks lodge for the spring prom. I never really played any sports.

I did not merely suck at biology. I also sucked at chemistry and physics. So how I thought I was going to just slide right into my delusion of being a medical missionary, healing bodies and saving souls, I have no idea. I figured the Lord would work a miracle. Helen McCorvey knew different.

I would read some of my creative writing out loud to Miz Mack's class. There would be a pause. She would get this little smile on her face. She knew. She knew who would be listening to hearts with a stethoscope and who would be pouring his heart out on the page.

So one day we went around the room and said where we were going to college and what we planned to study. "Vanderbilt—premed," said eighteen-year-old Stuart, the big sap. Helen McCorvey said nothing, but she got that knowing smile.

That smile said, "You really have no idea who you are, do you?" I ran my mouth to run for student body president. I ran my mouth on the speech and debate team. I had zero problems jumping up and speaking to twenty or two hundred; it didn't seem to matter.

But was I going to lean into my natural-born gift of blarney? Aw, hell no. I was doubling down on premed.

Then came bio 101 at Vandy. And chemistry. I never even made it to physics. Now they're just piling on. They had it in for me. Turns out in science, there's also math involved. Why was I not told of this? It hardly seems fair.

My huge humanitarian heart, bent on the Nobel Prize in medicine, was put though the meat grinder of Vandy's freshman gauntlet of weed-out courses. How many other potential Schweitzers were sidetracked to TV newsrooms to warn viewers of slime in the ice machine in segments called, "Eat, Drink, and Be Wary?" Countless I'm sure. It's a travesty, I tell you.

I did OK. I finally graduated after cramming four years into six. I lost a couple of years face down in a tepid puddle of beer somewhere between the frat house on Kensington and the Exit/ In on Elliston Place. Along the way, I learned words like "tepid." I learned not to say "lukewarm piss-water" in polite company, even if it's more accurate.

I have a bachelor's degree in English. What can you do with a BA in English? Nothing, and everything. My Uncle Harry, a career chemist at DuPont near Kinston, North Carolina, asked this same hacky question in the presence of my mom, who had heard just about enough of it. After all, my parents had poured enough money into my degree that they could have bought a condo in Panama City instead.

My Uncle Harry was the kind of hopeless romantic who bought an anniversary card for his wife that he liked so much, he took it back and gave it to her again every year. Exact same card. I don't think the poor woman ever got a new anniversary message. That's what I call message discipline. So when he sneered, "What's the boy gonna do with a degree in English—teach?" my mom quipped, "Well, for one thing, he'll write his wife a new anniversary card every year."

They say a little humor goes a long way to heal our hearts. I may be a healer yet, just not a doctor. Somewhere, Miz Mack is smiling.

"

A little humor goes a long
way to heal our hearts."

. . . .

My headshot taken by Emily Baxter
of We Are All Criminals.
Durham, North Carolina.

THE STRIPPER
SAID NOTHING

. . . .

The man with the gun did all the talking.

Fraternity house
Undisclosed location
1978

On Complicity:

A couple of frat boys took turns with the stripper. At least I *thought*
she was a stripper. I quickly learned stripping was just the start of
a live sex show. Some of the brothers found her through a cabbie
who knew her pimp. Her agent/security arrived at the frat house
on campus, a squat man with a gun in his waistband, in case things
got really out of hand.

  She was a white woman with shoulder-length hair. Brunette,
maybe? I couldn't swear to it. I couldn't pick the pimp out of a
lineup. But half a lifetime later, I could still name the brothers—at
least the two I saw—if I had to.

  Decades later, my friend Holly called these frats—with
their limitless liquor, blacked-out windows and toxic, choking
testosterone—"rape clubs." I don't know if what I witnessed was

a felony—let alone a rape. I only know it was wrong. My son had no interest in following his father and becoming a frat boy. I never even brought it up.

I didn't take a turn, but how much difference was there between those who did and those who cheered and those who stepped outside to keep from vomiting? And just because I was one of the few who walked out, does it somehow absolve me of the crime? Am I allowed to say, "It was a different time," or "Alcohol and drugs were involved," or "She was a free moral agent," or "What happens among the brothers is a sacred secret," to justify what happened? Seems to me we're living in the same time, generations later. The only difference now is we're lying about it in congressional testimony. Is it resolved? Not for me.

I stood in the back by the stairs, but the room was not so large or so dark that I couldn't see which brothers took a turn—at least while I was there. It wasn't what I had signed up for. I remember the lights on the impromptu stage. I remember the shouts and catcalls. I remember them giving one brother shit for his ineptitude, the gap between his bravado and his fumbling performance. I remember the cool and the dark outside, the thump of the music from inside. I remember I had company outside. I think I remember who. A number of us turned out to be gay.

The brothers wounded themselves, wounded each other, used sex to murder spirit. No crime is victimless. And in a real crime, there is never just one victim. The ripples go on and on, rolling down through generations until there is healing.

The "little sister" I was paired with in my own fraternity was sweet and smart, and we became friends, although we have not spoken in decades. What would she say if she knew what her big brother was up to on a Saturday night while she was studying in her dorm room? Is she an unwitting victim? Not like the stripper but still.

Revealing a secret long-buried carries a risk that I will tear open an old wound or create a new one. Some girls made it through unscathed. Am I creating harm by trying to own my shame? Or am I just assuaging my guilt by copping to old crimes? I am as sick as my secrets. So if I tell you one shameful secret and I'm a little less sick, so what? How does that help you? It doesn't help the stripper. It doesn't help my sisters, my brothers.

There is a critical distinction between an admission and an amend, between apology and reparation. An apology begins with acknowledging wrongdoing. It may end right there. An amend begins with acknowledging harm. It goes on to try to make it right.

But the harm does not end just because I acknowledge it.

An amend is not merely mumbling, "I'm sorry." An amend is not begging forgiveness. Forget forgiveness. This isn't about that.

First, I have to acknowledge what I did and that it caused harm. So I cannot make amends for what my brothers did. I have my own role. Neither am I throwing them under the bus to make myself look good or feel better. I am not the hero here. I am the supplicant.

An amend is two statements and a question. The statements without the question is not an amend. The question without waiting for the response is not an amend. The response without my acting on the response is not an amend. So here's how it goes:

- I was wrong. I hurt you.
- I apologize. I regret it.
- Is there anything I can do to make this right?

Takes maybe ten seconds. Then I shut up and listen intently.

The response may be, "There's nothing you can do," or "Go kill yourself," or "How dare you?" or "What the fuck are you talking about?" or "You have no right to say that," or "I'm not going to play your little game," or "You piece of shit." The response may be silence. Or a sharp slap, a gut punch, a swift kick in the nuts.

The listening without interruption or argument is always the beginning of the amend, of the attempt to set right the wrong, but it's rarely the end. The "living amend" may go on without end. It does not involve words. The amend goes on whether we are speaking or not. The amend begins when I change. It starts when I am no longer silent. My silence was my sin. My speaking the question aloud is the beginning of my amends. But it's hardly the end. The amend goes on after you read these words. After you talk back to me and I try to take in the full import of what you are saying. The amend is not a prepared statement, taking no questions. It's taking on the questions, living with them, having no answers, no defense, no way to placate you. It's simply to hear you and see you, and to change and grow as the result. This is my necessary work.

"

My amends begin when I change.
It starts when I am no longer
silent. My silence was my sin."

. . . .

Me and my soulmate, Lorraine Jivoff,
and Spooks the duckling (last seen in
Centennial Park). Vanderbilt University,
Nashville, Tennessee. Fall 1979. Photo
courtesy of Kats Smith Barry.

MEET CUTE

. . . .

"Aren't you gonna introduce us?"

Lorraine Jivoff
Carmichael Towers
Vanderbilt University
Nashville, Tennessee
September 1979

On Synchronicity

I used to joke that my nickname should have been "lesbian starter kit." My t-shirt should have read, "I flip straight women." After me, she wasn't just done with one man. She was done with *all* men. But if you think about it, Meg was just being true to herself. And if it hadn't been for Meg, I never would have met Lorraine.

I dated Meg sophomore year at Vandy. We fooled around. We lay in my bed in the dorm and put our hands all over each other and listened to Crosby, Stills, Nash & Young's *Our House* on vinyl. I really liked her, but it was nothing like when I met Lorraine. And I'm guessing it wasn't like when Meg met her wife.

Meg broke up with me. I was often the dumpee, not the dumper. We remained friends and hung out that fall. One day, she brought me by her suite in Carmichael Towers, and that's when I first laid eyes on Lorraine. She was wearing a pair of green army pants. She had short, dark hair and big, bright eyes, and ample curves.

"Aren't you gonna introduce us to your friend, Meg?" she kinda teased, with a big smile that lit me up. I became close friends with all of her suite mates. They all came to our wedding. But I'm getting ahead of myself.

One of those women who shared the suite was Kats Smith—later Kats Smith Barry—a talented photojournalist who was just learning her craft. Kats went on to work for a national startup called *USA Today* and flew with founder Al Neuharth around the Pacific on his "jetcapade," introducing the revolutionary idea of (gasp!) color photography in a newspaper! (For you youngsters out there, "newspapers" were a text-based analog form of news media printed on broad sheets of paper and distributed daily by people called "paperboys," or "newsies." They dropped these rolled up papers from trucks, or threw them from bikes onto doorsteps, or just stood in the streets waving them and shouting, "EXTRA!")

One gorgeous fall day in Nashville, Kats was outside the A-frame Episcopal church on campus snapping photos. She waved Lorraine and me over to stand side by side, just the two of us. I turned to her just after the last click of the Minolta and said something totally unlike me: "We'll show these to our kids someday." It sounded like a dumb pickup line. It probably was a dumb pickup line. But it worked. Man, did it work.

Instantly, I felt a jolt in the middle of my chest, the likes of which I have never felt before or since. It felt like someone or something struck a giant tuning fork in my heart, filling my ribcage with a pure musical tone resonating on and on. It turns out, she felt the same thing. Something way, way beyond my dumb words was going on.

The jolt said, "This is true. You have spoken the truth. You have spoken your fate into existence." In a line to meet a girl, I had connected with my soulmate. Lorraine and I started dating. And by dating, I mean we became inseparable.

We'd lock the door to the one bathroom for the suite of six women and play in the shower together till the water ran cold. With or without the shower, we could steam up a room. We'd go to dinner with others and just stare into each other's eyes, tuning out the world. It was obnoxious. We didn't care.

We'd stay in bed on Sundays till 4 p.m., then shower and go to Waxie's Pub (only because Rotier's wasn't open), and we'd order bacon cheeseburgers the size of your head, bushel baskets of fries, and pitchers of cold beer. We gave no thought to gluten, or trans fats, or grams of carbs. It was a simpler time.

We'd hang out in the pub on campus, the Overcup Oak, which has a balcony overlooking the trees and a long lawn, and live out halcyon days, with no thoughts of a salary, or a mortgage, or a 401(k). Like I said, obnoxious. Still don't care.

Lorraine sang in a campus Broadway troupe called "The Original Cast." They'd raise money with twenty-four-hour singathons, rolling a piano onto a plaza in the middle of campus and belting out show tunes till the break of dawn, singing themselves hoarse, their voices ragged, and finally collapsing drunk and happy in bed to sleep it off.

Lorraine has a strong, pure soprano voice. Once she sang "And This Is My Beloved" from the musical *Kismet* at the 1,104-seat Langford Auditorium while I stood in the back next to an ex of hers. He leaned over and said, "How does it feel to know she's singing that just for you?" Felt pretty fuckin' good.

We moved in together in a series of houses, duplexes, and apartments around Nashville till I finally graduated. I kept a second cheap rental to avoid confronting my mom with our "living in sin."

I would never have graduated had it not been for Lorraine. I would not have had the same career. We would not have had Erin and Glynis and Colleen and Jack. I would not be writing these words. And I would not have met Lorraine had it not been for Meg.

Meg works as a computer scientist now and lives in New England. We don't speak nearly often enough. We are still friends. We are still married—she to her wife, and me to mine. Kismet.

WATCH, LISTEN, AND LEARN
To hear Lorraine Jivoff tell her own story,
visit ManListening.com to view a video.

"

*It felt like someone or something
struck a giant tuning fork in
my heart, filling my ribcage
with a pure musical note,
resonating on and on."*

. . . .

Clockwise: Colleen (wincing), Erin, Jack,
Glynis, me, and Lorraine.
Photo courtesy of Michael
Harrison Photography.

THE REAL SEX TALK

. . . .

"Don't be so task-oriented."

Lorraine Jivoff
Girlfriend
Vanderbilt University
Nashville, Tennessee
1980

On Sex

I have never had sex with a virgin. I didn't have sex until I was twenty. I've had six partners in sixty years: a girlfriend, my fiancé (now wife), a one-night stand, and three poor choices. I have never had sex with more than one person at once. I have never had anal sex, pitching or catching. I have never had an STD. I have never had sex with a man, not that I haven't considered it. My most frequent lifelong sex partner is myself.

Any sex other than with my wife and possibly the girlfriend was transactional.

The sex with Lorraine was distinct. We would make out in the pouring rain before we ever had sex, and we've shared a bed long after sex passed.

With a few rare exceptions during my drinking, that relationship has been monogamous. Lorraine knows about those exceptions. In each case, she knows because I told her. I don't know if telling her was the right thing or not, but I did it. I do not recommend it. Some things she'd just as soon not know.

I guess she has forgiven me, but I know she has not forgotten. I know that it happened decades ago. I know I am completely capable of being selfish while clean and sober. I do not blame my infidelity on my drinking or vice versa. I own my wrongs. I address my guilt. I refuse to live with shame anymore.

Lorraine and I didn't have sex until three months after we met, which is a little surprising to me now because we were all over each other. I do not compare our sex life to anyone else's, not even our own. Comparison is a soul suck.

I was never a player.

I have not had sex outside my marriage in decades.

I do not believe prolonged flirting is healthy for me. I do not have affairs, even romantic ones. I recognize the distinction.

I delight in Lorraine's company. I love sharing adventures with her. When I travel without her, I miss her. She does not believe this. But physical affection is not my primary love language, nor is it hers.

The best thing Lorraine ever told me about sex was early on: "Don't be so task-oriented."

She kept asking me to give our son the sex talk. I never did. The closest I ever got was, "Try to be kind."

"

I own my wrongs. I address my guilt. I refuse to live with shame anymore."

. . . .

Dad checking the mailbox. Pea gravel
driveway. Hilltop Drive. Albany, Georgia.

HIGH DIVE INTO A DUMPSTER

. . . .

"Avoid black and white thinking."
Jean, Counselor
Psychological and Counseling Center
Vanderbilt University
Nashville, Tennessee
1981

On Suicide

Here is what Dad said: "School is your job."

Here is what I heard: "If you fail, you might as well kill yourself."

Here is what I recall Jean the therapist said: "Avoid black and white thinking."

I failed. So for the first time in my life, I planned to kill myself. First, I dropped out. I asked to leave Vanderbilt. Then I went back and failed and failed again. That's when Vanderbilt asked me to leave, at least for a semester. "Decide if you really want to be here." I had three years' worth of credits. I was three-fourths complete. And I felt like I had no future anywhere.

My peers had graduated. I felt left behind, out of sync, like something was wrong with me. And it was. I was suicidal. I felt responsible for my own unworthiness. In my worse moments, even now, I feel like I started life in a hole, in debt. And I never completely climbed out. I owed the world something I never got.

My dad paid for everything. On Christmas mornings, our living room looked like a game show studio, all lit up and filled with valuable prizes. He paid for trips to Europe, a private school-education, and then Vanderbilt. I am a portrait of white, male privilege.

I owed my dad my life and had defaulted. Time to pay up. So this was what I planned to give him. I would throw myself away by throwing myself off a building. It would have destroyed him, me destroying myself. It would have worked.

I lived in Carmichael Towers on West End Avenue, in the first of four high-rise dorms looking back toward the skyline of Music City, USA. I had a single room with a view. Looking up, the horizon twinkled with possibility. I did not look up. I looked down at a dumpster twelve floors below.

I did a physics problem over and over in my head. Could I gather enough momentum in this cramped space to break through the window and still hit the dumpster a dozen floors down? I was never good at physics. Or gathering momentum. Or diving, for that matter. This was my plan—to throw my life in a garbage bin. I didn't say it was a good plan, but it seemed like the only option at the time.

Inside that dorm room, I stayed up all night with the lights off, staring into the dark. It was December. I was supposed to go home and explain to my parents that I had failed again, flunked out this time. I curled into the fetal position and faced the block wall. I traced the right angles across and down in the mortar with my index finger, a binary choice, to be or not to be.

Around dawn, I put on clothes and walked down a dozen or so flights of grey concrete stairs. I never knew what surrender looked like. I gave up choosing and just kept walking. I chose to consider that meaning is only possible some steps hence, only when I can turn and look back. I walked slowly, step by step, out West End to St. Thomas, sat down, and then walked back again.

My dictionary app tells me "the capacity to act" is the ninth definition of "agency." You have to keep moving through eight layers of meaning just to get there.

I didn't call Jean until thoughts of suicide passed. When I really needed her, I didn't want to bother her. That's when she taught me that I needed to develop some way of coping, other than black-and-white thinking. The world is filled with failure. No real education occurs without it. It's all part of the lesson. Don't do something stupid.

"Hey," I say. "Can't spell 'stupid' without S-T-U!"

I waited tables at Dalt's in Lion's Head Village. I shacked up with Lorraine. I drank a lot. A bartender named Swig introduced me to the good people at 202 Friendship House within walking distance of campus on 23rd Avenue North. It was filled with clear-eyed, happy people. I didn't go back to that twelve-step clubhouse for eleven years, but Swig had planted a seed.

I graduated. I got a job in TV news. I got married. Three seismic changes in four months. We made my dad a granddad four times over. I eventually got sober. I was part of great teams of journalists that won three Peabody Awards. I raised smart kids.

I won a fellowship to Harvard. I got fired from the TV news and wrote this book you're reading. I've had a twinkling life that I could have never imagined on that dark night. I didn't know what I didn't know.

Last I checked, Jean is a practicing therapist in the DC area. My parents died knowing it all worked out OK. Lorraine and I are still married. The kids are mostly good.

Vanderbilt blew up the first of Carmichael Towers last summer. Being Vanderbilt, they sold t-shirts and mugs and engraved bricks. I took a pass. Instead I hired my friend Rodney to shoot a little video of the dramatic implosion. Drone shots and cell phone video appeared on YouTube. In a plume, the walls fell. I was far away, reading a book.

"

The world is filled with failure. No real education occurs without it."

. . . .

Me and Steve Hartman at my going away
party from WTOL-TV. Kelsey's Saloon.
Toledo, Ohio. September 1987.
Photo courtesy of Rodney King.

THE MAN IN THE BOTTLE

. . . .

"Are you kidding?"

Tammy Bell,
Relapse-prevention specialist
Charlotte, North Carolina
1994 (recounted 2015)

On Abandonment

Lorraine told me she was pregnant. I couldn't hide my fear. She made $11,000 that year, 1984. I made $14,000. Before delivery, she quit her job. I hadn't planned on this. I couldn't support us, much less a baby. She sat me down outside City Hall in Jackson, Mississippi, where I'd landed my first job in local TV news. I interviewed men running for president: Jesse Jackson, John Glenn, Walter Mondale. At a news conference, I asked George H. W. Bush a question that I clipped out of *Parade* magazine. I fancied myself a local celebrity. But when she told me I was going to be a father, I was just a scared little boy. She cried.

Men leave. It's what we do best. We go to sea. We go to war. We go to work. Go go go. I go to the bar. That's where I go. The night Erin was born, I put on a tuxedo and brought Lorraine a bottle of champagne, and then I left her in Woman's Hospital in Flowood, Mississippi. I bought drinks all round at the George Street Grocery in Jackson. I had fathered a child. That's just biology. But I was no kind of dad.

I fell completely in love with that little girl, but she didn't make it easy. She screamed loud enough to peel paint. I would check her diaper. Get her a bottle. Hold her. Rock her. Walk the floor with her. Didn't matter. She'd scream for hours. Shaken baby syndrome is awful, but after months of little sleep, I understood how it happens. They say colicky babies are smart. Erin turned out smart as a whip.

Lorraine is from Syracuse, New York. In Mississippi, she never seemed to fit in. If she heard it once, she heard it a thousand times: "You're not from around here, are you?" We moved to Ohio—WTOL Toledo 11. Erin screamed less. She was cute as a bug. Lorraine took care of her 24/7. I worked. I made appearances for family dinner. I drank.

I'd go to Kelsey's Saloon at Michigan and Washington in downtown Toledo. I'd found a press bar, just like the one on George Street. I got pulled over by a cop one night just around the corner from Kelsey's for running a red light. "Have you had anything to drink?" the cop asked. "Couple of beers," I said, by which I meant a couple of pitchers. He gave me a ticket for the red light. I drove home and kept drinking. In no way do I excuse drinking and driving. But I lived it for years.

I once met a woman named Emily Baxter who formed a group called "We Are All Criminals." She takes photos of the hands of mostly white people holding signs hand-lettered with the felonies we'd gotten away with. Mine is easy—habitual drunk driving.

Addiction is a disease. Drunk driving is a crime. I am afflicted. And I am guilty. I just never got caught.

We moved again—back to Nashville. I got Lorraine pregnant again. I was following a presidential candidate named Al Gore through the snows of Iowa and New Hampshire. It's a wonder I was home long enough for the conception. This time, there were no tears. By then I earned $40,000 a year. But I didn't stop drinking.

I'd walk across the street from work at WKRN-TV to La Fiesta of Mexican Food, and Wayne, the owner, would grunt a greeting, and my beer would hit the bar before my butt hit the barstool. I'd hold court for hours, smoking cigarettes and bitching about the bosses. Lorraine would feed, bathe, and change the girls, and tuck them in with a story, but no daddy time.

"Why don't you just call me?" she'd ask. "Why don't you just let me know you're going to be late for dinner?" Fair question. The real answer? Because I'd rather hear her complaining about my drinking after than before. It was a buzzkill.

When home, I'd weave a path between the couch and a fifth of cheap scotch or a half gallon of cheap vodka. Some rounds into this Lorraine would ask a simple question I found impossible to understand: "Don't you think you've had enough?" I could not even parse the question to get to the basic concept. Enough? What is that? Like my biological father before me, I could chase "enough" into an asylum, a prison, and an early grave.

I now regard the question "Don't you think you've had enough?" as a kind of pre-Al-Anon zen koan—a question that's not really a question, but an unsolvable puzzle designed to short circuit the brain of its target into sudden enlightenment. Something like, "What is the sound of one hand clapping?" It didn't work. I remained unenlightened. Not woke. Not even waking.

Decades into sobriety, I once made the mistake of bragging to a specialist in the pathology of abandonment that I had never abandoned *my* family like my biological father abandoned us.

"Are you kidding?" she said. "You abandoned them right there. You abandoned them right in your own home."

I wanted a trophy as "Daddy of the Decade" for passing out in my own bed.

Abandoners abandon. It's what we do. I just can't pretend it's OK.

WATCH, LISTEN, AND LEARN

To hear Tammy Bell talk about addiction and recovery, visit ManListening.com to view a video.

"

Lorraine would ask a simple question I found impossible to understand: 'Don't you think you've had enough?'"

. . . .

My daughter Erin looking up at the
TV when she heard my
voice on WTOL Toledo 11.
Sylvania Township, Ohio. 1986.

SHE SLAPPED
THE SHIT OUT OF ME

. . . .

Producer
WKRN-TV
Nashville, Tennessee
Circa 1991

On Toxic Masculinity

She stepped over and slapped me hard across the face. I shut
up. The other men at the conference table either laughed or
stopped laughing.

We were sitting in a little side conference room off the
WKRN-TV newsroom set, one with sliding glass patio doors, and
fluorescent lights, and removable, square floor tiles with all the
cables snaking beneath. The group was all men. I can't recall her
name to save me. I'll never forget the slap.

We men were having lunch and talking as men sometimes do. It
was not a locker room. I've never spent much time in locker rooms
having never been much of a jock. Confident men do not feel
compelled to prove themselves with such talk.

I was not a particularly confident man, although I played one
on TV.

I did not address the comment to her. Had you asked me, I would have just said she walked in at precisely the wrong time, at the punchline of an unfunny joke that no one asked me to tell.

I tell stories. That I can do. So I was telling a story, making an observation about a whole class of women based on a sample of one, which is never good science, but this was a story. I didn't address the comment at her, but I didn't stifle it either. My words had an unintended audience.

"Oh God, Dad," my youngest daughter Colleen said. It was decades later when I told her the story of the slap. "I don't *even* want to think what you said."

"Well, I'd rather tell you than have you imagine it," I said. "Because whatever you imagine is far worse than what I actually said."

One time, more than twenty years later, I stopped the car in Chapel Hill near the University of North Carolina. Colleen was riding in the backseat with the family. I turned just in time to see her flip off three laughing boys ambling up Franklin Street. Flipped 'em off with both hands, more like fists than not.

"What was that?" I asked.

"Nothing," she said. "Just drive."

"What?" I said. "What did they say?"

"Nothing," she said. "Just forget it."

She never did tell me what they said. And I never told her what I said. But we each got the gist. I said what I said. The woman slapped me hard across the face. I never said it again. There was no HR interview, no disciplinary action, no lawsuit, and no criminal charge. It felt unresolved. I feel like I owe her an apology. I feel like I owe her a debt of gratitude.

I told the story to my small group in a leadership class at the John F. Kennedy School of Government, including women from Europe and South America. They seemed aghast to me. I couldn't tell if it was because they imagined me offensive or the slapper as violent. Americans.

I asked my oldest daughter, Erin, in a text message to explain terms to me terms like "microaggression," and "intersectional feminism." A millennial, she gets tired of being tutor to a boomer by text. She has a job. The dots undulated for a moment on the small screen. She was responding. "We've been over this," she typed, thumbs flying.

"Toxic masculinity" I get. I guess I get it 'cause I got it. Sticks and stones. That's how I grew up. Then I learned how words start wars. And even if the war is never fought, the slap never returned, the toxins accumulate. The poison builds.

Drinking at La Fiesta of Mexican Food (now closed)
with Jennifer Walsh (now deceased).
Early 1990s. Murfreesboro Road.
Nashville, Tennessee.

THE BOTTOM

. . . .

"A person filled with self-loathing."

Nancy, recovering codependent
Anuvia Prevention and Recovery
Charlotte, North Carolina
1993 (recounted 2017)

On Alcoholism

Towards the end, it's not a big party. It's a party of one. As I
approached the bottom, it was more pathology, self-punishment.
It's akin to self-harm. Wrist-slicing for cowards. Suicide in slow
motion. Take the anesthesia. Then wake up bleeding. What
happened? I can't remember. In blackouts, the brain records
nothing. There is no memory to retrieve—not with all
the hypnosis or sodium pentothol in the world.

At the best moments, it's like a bad flu every morning—the
shits, the sweats, and the shakes. At the worst, I wanted to die but
didn't have the gumption. One guy I knew in recovery relapsed
and ran his car into a tree. It caught fire. Someone told me it was
an accident. Didn't sound accidental to me. He's dead either way.

Bright, good looking, professional, and rarely shared his ugly inner turmoil. Was mostly like, "I'm fine, great!"

My father's death certificate, signed by his family doctor, spelled out the cause of his demise—"acute alcoholism." Next line: "As a result of excessive drinking." Duh. Circular reasoning there, doc. Then the coroner told me my sister's cause of death was "multiple organ failure." What the fuck does that even mean? She died because her heart and brain stopped? But what makes them stop?

My father was forty-six. My sister got a decade or so more. The guy in the flaming car? Might have made it to sixty. Any way you cut it, abbreviated lives. What's the saying? "First you go to hell. Then you die." Hell is not other people. Hell is completely alone, cut off from everything and everyone.

You think you can locate hell on a map. It's under a bridge, behind a dumpster, in a van down by the river. Oh, no. Hell can be beside your swimming pool, bought and paid for. Hell can be at the country club, requiring a straw for the first drink because you're shaking so badly, or in your SUV in line to pick up the kids, water bottle filled with wine.

My road to Margaritaville used to go to a place with easy music and soft breezes, twinkling lights, and young women. Years later, I was on the same road, bending the same elbow, drinking from the same salted rim. But there were no steel drums, no girls, and especially no light.

Instead, I'd come to, alone in the dark. Oh, there could be a whole crowd around me. But I was alone. I was cut off from Lorraine and from our daughters, cut off from Mom and Dad and sister, at the bottom of a bottle. I could see their warped images. But I could not touch them, and they could not reach me.

Fueled with vodka, I would get in our Honda Civic late at night after Lorraine had gone to bed and drive around Shelby Park in east Nashville, down by the Cumberland River. Drinking and thinking. Thinking and drinking. Where was I going? Nowhere. On a winding route, mercifully ending up back in my driveway, still in one piece, still in the dark.

I call it step zero. You go round and round. You spiral down. You get nowhere. Each morning, the same hell. You can stay here for a lifetime. Most people like me never make it out, at least not for long. In my bar, they never took down the Christmas lights. Seemed like too much trouble. They could just unplug them and leave them dark. It wasn't festive, just sad.

Many of the twelve steps have observations and prayers and promises. For step zero, the observation sounds something like, "This shit has got to stop." The prayer? "God get me out of this. I swear I'll never do it again." That's lets-make-a-deal, not surrender. And the promise? It just gets worse.

If the bottom really is the bottom, it's a blessing. The bottom is only the bottom in hindsight. For some, death is the bottom, with no place to go but up.

Even some people in long-term recovery don't know there are two sides to the twelve steps, a kind of yin-yang approach. One side is manly, filled with imperative commands and repeated variations of the word *you:* "Sit your ass down and listen. Take the cotton out of your ears and put it in your mouth. You've got nothing we want." The other is a motherly we approach: "It's OK, honey. We've all been there. Can I get you a tissue?" I lean toward the sacred feminine, but one approach may be as effective as another depending on the person.

The single best thing I've ever learned about alcoholism/
addiction/substance use disorder, whatever the current term of art,
was from a woman on the "yang" side. You know. Your Al-Anon,
your ACOA, codependent-no-more crowd.

Her name's Nancy. She has tons of experience with the
disorder—father, ex-husband, friends, the whole ringer. She said,
"Show me any active alcoholic, and I'll show you a person filled
with self-loathing."

When I shaved before the bathroom mirror, I wouldn't look
myself in the eye. I fucking hated that guy. He'd lie to me every
day. He'd say today was gonna be different.

"

The prayer? 'God get me out of this. I swear I'll never do it again.' That's lets-make-a-deal, not surrender."

. . . .

I was a know-it-all newcomer.
Illustration by Joel Kweskin.

THE MESSENGER
& THE MESSAGE

. . . .

"Why don't you get your ass up?"

Anonymous woman
Twelve-Step Clubhouse
Nolensville Rd.
Nashville, Tennessee
1993

On Identifying

We met in a white house on Nolensville Road, which runs
outbound on a map about five o'clock on Nashville's south side. The
old twelve-step clubhouse has long since been bulldozed. The site is
unmarked. It's just past the Speedy Cash on your right after I-440
and before the Hispanic megachurch Iglesia Una Esperanza Viva.

In a building, about where the striped blacktop parking spaces
are now, the usual twelve steps and twelve traditions hung on the
wall. There were portraits of patron saints Bill and Dr. Bob, hung
with the reverence usually reserved for the pope or MLK. Only
all these wall hangings were sepia-toned from untold cigarettes
yellowing hallowed spiritual law, like the ten commandments hung
in a bowling alley. I'd be shocked if the clubhouse met building codes.

Seemed to me like the whole structure was held together by nicotine and despair.

A large, open front room had tables down the middle with chairs around them and lined up against the wall. My group met in the back room to try to escape the stink of burnt tobacco and the insistence that second-hand smoke was a necessary hazing to get sober.

I never saw a civil war like the one when a group decided to go nonsmoking. To some, a meeting without cigarettes was like saying you could have a spiritual awakening without wretched black coffee in tiny, Styrofoam cups, made drinkable only by upending a sugar dispenser or opening five packs at once, creating a sticky grey sludge to then spill on the floor.

The Sunday morning meeting in the much smaller back room, which may have once been a porch, was packed elbows to armpits with people standing just outside a cracked window and others spilling out the back door, listening intently to the shares. You'd best get there early, or you'd never get standing room, let alone a seat.

I was an eager-beaver newcomer. I wanted to live. I'd gotten a taste of freedom and was bound and damned determined to keep it. So I had a front seat at the table. Thinking I would show off my newfound brilliance, I proceeded to share my problem in the guise of teaching these poor rubes my personal tips for sobriety, all while making it clear I was never as bad off as them.

"I've never been to jail, never been divorced, never had a DUI, never been fired, never wrecked a car, never hit my wife ..." I went on at length in Neverland, doing my best to exclude myself and alienate my audience by the moment. Never, never, never. That's when she said it.

"Then why don't you get your ass up?" the blonde to my left spoke up. "We could use your chair." She got a laugh.

"Because," I lectured Blondie, doubling down. "The only requirement for membership is a desire to stop drinking." Boom. Mic drop. I'd rather be right than learn any day.

It took a few steps before I began to see exactly how and why I showed my ass that day. And whether you call it by four syllables (narcissism), or by three (selfishness), or by two (ego), or by one (pride), it's all the same twisted root.

I heard that woman tell her story later on. She was from southern California. She'd hang out poolside in her bikini like a lawn ornament, blind drunk and ignoring her little girl while she went under water once, twice, three times, and almost drowned. I never lived in California. I never once wore a bikini. No one would consider me arm candy. But I've ignored my little girl in a pool while she stepped off into the deep water and bobbed for dear life. Thank God someone was paying attention.

"I was convinced God didn't love skinny little whores," she said. And my heart broke open. My eyes watered. I felt huge compassion for this woman. And if she was lovable in her wretchedness, maybe I was too.

"When your heart is broken, when your heart has cracks in it, that's how the light gets in," so said the poet Ellen DeGeneres. I'm pretty sure some of that light is pouring out. I go looking for the light in the wilderness. I look for it in art and temple and pilgrimage. I found it on a folding chair in a cramped back porch behind a smoke-filled room with a cup of grey coffee and the help of a skinny blonde woman from southern California. I can't even recall her name.

WATCH, LISTEN, AND LEARN

To hear stories of women who have recovered from addiction, visit ManListening.com for podcasts with women like Tina, Robin, and Jan.

My daughters Glynis and Erin at the
North Carolina Zoo. Asheboro,
North Carolina. Late '90s.

MAKING AMENDS TO FIVE- AND EIGHT- YEAR-OLD GIRLS

. . . .

Small nods.

Erin Jivoff Watson & Glynis Jivoff Watson
Daughters
1410 Gartland Ave.
Nashville, Tennessee
Fall 1993

On Amends

The girls had this ceramic piggy bank with a slot in its back and a rubber stopper in the belly. I would "borrow" (steal) bills and coins from my kids to run out the back door and down the alley behind our East Nashville bungalow, and buy six packs of tall boys at the market on the corner of Woodland and 14th streets, the one where the cop shot the hostages as they ran out that one time. I digress.

Bottom line: I stole from my daughters to support my alcohol addiction.

So I sat the girls down when Erin was about eight and Glynis about five, and I said, "You know Daddy used to drink lots of beer, right?"

Eyes down.

"And you know Daddy is not drinking beer anymore?"

Small nods.

"So I used to take money from your piggy bank to buy the beer. And now I want to pay you back," I kinda blurted. "So we have to figure up how much I owe you."

"Ten thousand dollars," Erin suggested helpfully.

"By the time you graduate college, you'll get it all back and more," I said.

They're both married, working women now, with husbands and dogs. Over two dozen years I wrote checks for orthodontia and checks for tuition and checks for weddings. When they set a date to get married, I wrote them each a check for $10,000. It wasn't enough.

"

I would 'borrow' (steal) from my kids to buy six packs of tall boys."

. . . .

My daughter Glynis. Walden Pond.
Massachusetts. October 2007.

THE MEAN TEACHER

. . . .

"Life is HARD!"

Glynis Jivoff Watson
501 Cayman Ave.
Holly Springs, North Carolina
Fall 1995

On Suffering

Glynnie's kindergarten teacher was a hugger; she loved on those kids. She was sweet as chess pie. It was more like pre-K than kindergarten. Then we moved. Her first-grade teacher was a cold shower—treated her like a fifth grader. She was trying to get the kids ready for something. No more hugging. No more sweetie pie. Put your book bag in the cubby and sit down.

Glynis always was sensitive. You're not supposed to pick favorites among your kids, and I don't. I'm just going to make a statement. Genetically, in both body type and disposition, Glynis is more like me and my birth mother than she is like her mother and her mother's mother.

She's fat. I use the word because she does. She doesn't shy away from it.

You look at my mother and her sister and her brothers. Glynis is more their body type. I won't say "fat," but they might. My sister, who died last year, had a gastric bypass. My uncle, who is practically my age, did too. My brother has been giving himself insulin shots for years. And I'm no skinny mini. Six feet tall. 260 pounds. BMI 35. Waist 40 pinched in a bit.

One day after first grade, Glynis came home from school and collapsed on her bed sobbing. She missed the hugs and constant reassurance of kindergarten. Even before school she seemed to feel her feelings more deeply than the other kids. She'd be inconsolable.

In between the gasps for air, she blurted out, "LIFE IS HARD." (Sob, sob, sob.) "LIFE IS HAAAARD!"

I couldn't suppress a laugh. She didn't seem to take offense. She brightened a bit.

"Congratulations, Glynis," I said. "It took the Buddha a lot longer than you to figure that out."

Twenty years later, Glynis came out of the dressing room sobbing in great heaving gasps like the little girl she once was. She had been trying on dresses for her wedding. She arranged everything else: venue, photographer, caterer. Check, check, and check. She put off the hard part till last.

But I didn't understand the sobbing. I can't pretend I did. The dressmaker specialized in large women. Wasn't he used to this sort of thing? Couldn't he make it stop? Say just the right thing?

"Leave her alone," he said. "This happens a lot."

At least that's what I imagine he said. I wasn't there. She went with her mother. That was her gift. That's how that works.

Being a reporter by trade, smart me decided to ask my daughter, "Why were you so upset?"

This isn't word for word, but I'll sum it up. "Dad, you have no idea what it's like to try to find clothes as a woman, let alone as a fat woman."

She's right of course. So a year or two later I decided to turn on the recorder and interview her about it for my podcast. Maybe I would have an epiphany or at least develop a little compassion. Glynis was cheerful and obliging for the old man.

For a man who prides himself on listening without interruption, or unsolicited advice, or argument, I sucked. It was unlistenable. I don't think I've ever been able to stomach listening to a whole hour of that chat. I'll never air it.

I cut her off. I changed the subject. I tried to get to the point, by which I mean my point. Whatever the hell that was, it wasn't listening.

"I'm not saying what you want me to say," she said.

It's hardest to listen to those we love. This is just science. It doesn't help that Glynis did not want to talk about her sobbing, but about patriarchal oppression, the male-dominated fashion industry, and how bras never fit. I am the patriarch. I run the show. That's how I do. Father God made it that way; have I not mansplained this to you?

Now I wanted to be all TV Dr. Phil and play out conflict, climax, and resolution on tape, and send her home with an aphorism and a gift bag. That wasn't happening.

In her years between the ages of eight and twenty-eight, I lectured and schooled and cajoled and criticized Glynis' diet and lack of exercise to mold her into Gramma Natalie on her mother's side or Great Grandmother Esther on my father's. None of it helped her. It was just nagging—pointless at best but usually counterproductive. She is who she is, and I finally just broke down and loved her for herself.

I don't make any comments about her menu selection at the restaurant. I don't push the soup and salad like a bad waiter. I don't ask whether she and her husband are walking on the greenway. I invite her to lunch, let her pick the restaurant, and choose her meal like the grown woman she is. We get along much better this way.

Life is hard enough on its own.

> "
> *Dad, you have no idea what it's like to try to find clothes as a woman, let alone as a fat woman.*"

....

Hugging and smooching Colleen and Jack.
University City. Charlotte, North Carolina.
November 2007.

BETTER THAN PLANNING

. . . .

"Awww. Look at that cute little face!"

Lorraine Jivoff
501 Cayman Ave.
Holly Springs, North Carolina
Winter 1995

On Planning

I'm not a big believer in planning. I've never used planners:
wedding, retirement, or funeral. Maybe it's just my experience
with the myth of control. Maybe it's all the Presbyterian stuff
about predestination. Maybe it was waking up to how much some
combination of DNA, trauma, and grace dictates our fate. Maybe
it's from trying to manage it all before final, complete surrender.

The wildest ride? The greatest delusion? Family planning. Do
you even know my family? Trust me—I could never have planned
this. Not with mathematical precision or wild hallucination,
not with Excel spreadsheets or taking ayahuasca. I owe my very
existence to a crazy tragicomedy. My mother met my father at the
largest mental institution in America, where she was a nursing
student and he was a patient. One of the drunks who ran the

hospital, which actually recruited its doctors from among the patients, thought it'd be a swell idea for the male patients to have a weekly dance with the young, pretty nurses. I can assure you no woman had final say in this barn dance. My father first laid eyes on my mother—her blonde hair pulled back in a ponytail over her white nurse's uniform—doing the "bunny hop" in the Georgia State Lunatic Asylum, as it was once known. My people!

She dated him, got pregnant by him, lost him, lost me, got sucked in by him again, snuck over to Alabama, and got hitched to him on a New Year's Eve by a probate judge with a quick blood test. Then she had two more kids by him, divorced him, took him back (again), and *RE*married him! Does any of this sound remotely like planning?

Then there's my own family non-planning. One night, after too much wine and soft-shell crab at Walker's Drive-In in Jackson, Mississippi, Lorraine got pregnant with Erin. On news of the conception, I dissociated, having an out-of-body experience, behaving as though we were exempt from basic biology.

Come to think of it, Lorraine and I never once used a condom, which is to say I left birth control, IUD, the pill, and all matters family up to her. I was only good for a few minutes of huffing and puffing. Hey, she stayed. She always wanted kids.

The month after George H. W. Bush was elected, daughter number two was born. We planned for Lorraine to name her Kiely (KEE-lee) if it was a girl, and I would name it Nick or Ben or Jack if it was a boy. No sooner than baby girl number two was born, I went back on my end of the deal. I fought Lorraine over the name until they forced us to fill out the birth certificate. Then I got my way. You're welcome, Glynis. I really don't see you as a Kiely.

In the seven years that followed, Lorraine had one very early miscarriage. She was disappointed but not despondent. That was it on the pregnancy front. I figured we were done. I just assumed we would have the two girls.

Then moments after letting me know that my dad's mom had died, Lorraine left the pee stick on my dresser. It had a plus sign. One generation passes. Another arrives. I grieved the loss of Mama Annie—my granny. But I was elated at the thought of a new baby. I was finally sober and ready to be a decent dad. Third time's the charm. Glynis had a baby sister, Colleen, and Erin got stuck with years of unpaid babysitting.

That's when I said, "OK, it's time. Snip, snip. I'm going in for a vasectomy." Here's what Lorraine said, "Awww! Look at that cute little face! Why don't we just see what happens?" She was one of six kids. I was one of two adoptees with a mom and dad who for whatever reason couldn't conceive. We planned not to plan, but we were open to a fourth. I just didn't think it would happen.

Oh, it happened. Two years later, Lorraine was pregnant and pushing forty. My mother's mother was in her forties when she last gave birth, and it was grueling work to carry the pregnancy to term, and excruciating work to deliver a huge boy, my Uncle William. I know all this because my mother helped deliver her baby brother, all while she was pregnant with me. That's right. My mother and her mother were pregnant at the same time.

As far as Lorraine's labor and delivery went, my son, Jack, was a ten pounder, the size of a bowling ball, and Lorraine had not so much as a baby aspirin for the pain.

I got a vasectomy the same year. I was a great big baby about it. I took all the anesthesia they would give.

"This feels like a violation," I whined. "It's embarrassing."

"Oh, yeah?" Lorraine said. "Try stirrups."

"This is gonna hurt!" I complained, still looking for a little sympathy.

"Oh, yeah?" Lorraine said. "Try labor."

Years later at the dinner table, one of the older kids picked up on my inside joke of all our happy accidents and turned to her sibling saying, "You weren't planned." As if she was.

From the head of the table I shut it down. "Hey!" I said. "Listen to me. As far as I'm concerned, none of you were planned." Four heads turned and four pairs of young eyes cut back to mom, the final word on all things family.

She said, "I planned all of you."

WATCH, LISTEN, AND LEARN

To hear Stuart talk about the miracle of childbirth with an OB-GYN who has birthed thousands, go to ManListening.com and look for the podcast with Dr. Octavia Cannon.

"

Here's what I said:
'I'm getting a vasectomy.'

Here's what she said:
'Why don't we just see
what happens?'

Oh, it happened."

. . . .

IS
A   BC Y
EVEN
LISTENING

Graffiti. Coffee house bathroom.
Chicago, Illinois. 2017

WHAT IS HEARD

. . . .

"Your girls are SO cute!"

Store clerk
Savannah, Georgia
Spring 1998

On Sexuality

It was spring break, but it was cold in Savannah. We met with
Mom and Dad, and they made a reservation for our girls to take
a boat ride to see dolphins. It was pretty basic. The captain of the
skiff would trace gentle curves along the stream through the marsh.
At a point where he knew there'd be dolphins, he'd cut the engines
and bang the side of the boat to call over one he knew by name.
When the smiling dolphin face broke the surface, he'd toss out a
bit of chum, a fishy snack for this fellow air breather. Kinda like
showtime at the aquarium, only "in the wild."

It was colder still on the water, but we hadn't packed clothes for
this. So I took the girls to one of those riverfront tourist shops for
overpriced sweatshirts. The saleswoman (you can't say "shopgirl")
was cute, young, and sexy, a triple threat. She was wearing a skirt. I
have a vague recollection of her legs, not her face.

We were the only ones in the shop. It was early. So she came out from behind the counter, past the cut glass figurines, and pawed through stacks of sweatshirts with us.

I'd squatted down in a catcher's stance to show a shirt to my girls when the young woman leaned over, extra friendly like, and said, "Your girls are SO cute." A wave of her perfume crashed over us. I felt suddenly invisible.

Now wait. Did she say, "YOUR girls are so cute?" Or "YOU girls are so cute?" Which was it? Was the syrupy compliment girl to girl? Or woman to man? I remember it as "YOUR girls."

The girls were in front of me, and I crouched between them. They were like a barrier, a couple of football linemen sealing the gap. I remember hugging them to me.

We humans usually have some recollection of the first time we have sex, fumbling, messy, and painful as it may be. I was with KT in her dorm room sophomore year. We'd been reading the Bible. She'd had sex with her high school math teacher. She'd had sex with a couple of football players. I'd had sex with a poster of Farrah Fawcett from Spencer Gifts in the mall. But for about six months that year, I found girls attracted to me. Then the window closed. Good thing I met Lorraine in those months.

In that moment in the shop in Savannah, I abruptly felt nonsexual, existing only in relation to my daughters. I felt like the safe dad who passed an idle moment before a sale. I never really want to be the safe dad. I always want sex to at least be a possibility. I want to be just a little bit dangerous. I want to be seen in full. Yet I didn't see this young woman. And she didn't see me.

Maybe she was hitting on me. Maybe she came out from behind the counter to talk to me. Maybe it really was "your" not "you." This seems unlikely. But I could also see how a pair of cute daughters might make a man seem more attractive, like a puppy in a Tinder pic. I'm not proud of any of these thoughts.

What does it say that decades later I still remember this moment in a shop in Savannah? What does it say that a man who calls himself a reporter can't get a simple quote right? If the moment was so damn important that I committed it to memory, why can't I remember if she said "you" or "your?"

Years later, my wife and I sat on a swing in a park at night, our girls long gone. I said, "You're beautiful."

She sniffed, "Cashiers at the grocery store look straight through me. I'm invisible."

"I get it," I said. "But do you believe I believe you're beautiful?'

There is what is said, and then there is what is heard. What is heard is all that matters.

Roberta Baskin with a photo of
her long-lost father, Alan Baskin.
Manassas, Virginia. 2017.

A PAIN IN MY ASS

. . . .

"FIND YOUR MOTHER!"

Roberta Baskin
Mentor
Hilton Hotel Lobby
St. Petersburg, Florida
1998

On Searching

Roberta Baskin swooped in as a kind of guardian angel for me—and by guardian angel, I mean colossal pain in my ass. Roberta will get an idea in her head and pursues it with such dogged stubbornness that the universe rearranges itself to bend to her will. That looks ridiculous as I type it, but it's true. This was all to the better for me. Her ideas were bigger and better than my own.

Roberta got the idea that she and her husband should go together to Harvard for a mid-career fellowship for journalists. This was not done. The Nieman Foundation for Journalism didn't give fellowships to both spouses. But they did for her and Jim.

Then she got the idea I should go to Harvard at mid-career. And she would … not … stop. The woman was relentless. She had a kind of single-minded obsession I have not witnessed before or since.

I met Roberta at the Poynter Institute for Media Studies in St. Petersburg, Florida, somewhere around 1998. She was visiting faculty at a one-week seminar on investigative reporting. I went to that seminar once as a student and a couple of times as visiting faculty, which was kind of a joke because many of the students were more accomplished at the craft than I was. They schooled me, not the other way around.

I knew Roberta's reputation from Investigative Reporters and Editors (IRE), our professional group based at Mizzou, the University of Missouri. She served on the board and talked me into running for the board after her. And with IRE, it is public service. You're asked to pay your own way to board meetings and carve out hours and hours and hours from your already extensive workweek to help your colleagues.

Sure, a certain cachet comes with the position, but you've gotta do it because you love the work. And in my case, I loved the work because I loved and admired the people who did the work. The true believers. The ones who thought journalism served people, not dollars or corporations, status or ego. Roberta was one. She was a leader in that group.

She quit her job as an investigative correspondent at CBS after she got sideways with the network president over the network incorporating the Nike swoosh logo on journalists' jackets during its coverage of the Winter Olympics. Now the issue of TV selling out seems like a done deal. But Roberta sacrificed a plum job over it.

Roberta worked at ABC TV on the news magazine show *20/20*. She worked for Bill Moyers at PBS. She did a brief stint as head of the Center for Public Integrity, founded by one of my all-time heroes, Chuck Lewis, who walked away from a job at *60 Minutes* to spread the gospel of speaking truth to power.

Now, Roberta took an interest in me. In my career. Why? I don't really know. She believed in me. She thought I had talent. Hell, *I* didn't believe in me! I didn't think I had that kind of talent.

We were drinking late one night in the lobby of the Hilton Hotel across the street from the ballpark where the St. Louis Cardinals once played spring training games. My fellow reporters usually drank beer. I had soda water with lemon. Roberta was going on and on about the Nieman Fellowship, the one at Harvard, how I HAD to do it. It took me ten years, two attempts, and Roberta herself on the selection committee (abstaining from the vote, but making no secret of her support for me) to finally get in.

But Roberta and I had something else in common. She had gone in search of her father. She had used her investigative reporting skills to find and reunite with a parent at midlife. Growing up, Roberta's mother told her that her father was dead. Turns out she meant dead to *her*. Alan Baskin was actually very much alive and living in the Caribbean, running a dive shop in Tortola called "Baskin in the Sun."

Roberta called on all her investigative reporting skills, even a source in federal law enforcement, to find her father. Turns out he caught a federal charge at one point, but was now living happily abroad in a blue-watered tropical paradise. She can tell her own story much better and has in *Washingtonian* magazine, and I think she's now slowly writing her own book. Long story short: she reunited with him and really got to know and love him before he died. Matter of fact, as they all knew he was dying, Roberta developed a kind of online eulogy before the fact, giving her father's dive customers a chance to share memories and say thanks. A few of those posting in gratitude: the legendary CBS anchor Walter Cronkite, the great writer George Plimpton, and the comedian David Brenner.

This is a roundabout way of saying when I told Roberta about my adoption and the search for my birth mother, Roberta's eyes got even bigger than usual. "You MUST find her!" Roberta was big on "musts." Everything was an imperative with her. It MUST happen. She would make it so.

I remember this very clearly now, because I walked out of that hotel lobby to fly back to WRAL and North Carolina with Roberta's overwhelming command ringing in my head, my biggest investigative report, the investigation of a life, my life.

"FIND YOUR MOTHER!" she said. It took five more years, but I did.

WATCH, LISTEN, AND LEARN

To hear Roberta tell her own story, visit ManListening.com to view a video.

*"She believed in me. Hell,
I didn't believe in me."*

. . . .

My blood family that I didn't know. Brother
Andy Schmid, father Scott Schmid, and
sister Esther Schmid. Commerce, Georgia.
Late 1960s.

THE QUESTION

. . . .

"Why are you so angry with him?"
Holly Williams, Nieman Fellow
Harvard University
Lippmann House
Cambridge, Massachusetts
April 2008

On Resentment

I blamed him. I blamed my bio father for abandoning me. I didn't blame my mother. Maybe it's because I met her, because she is one of my best friends. And he died before I found out who he was. But I knew he was a drunk. Totally self-involved. An abandoner. So I blamed him.

My brother told me a story that one of our uncles told him. I have no idea if the story is true. But it's true that he told it. So take it for what it's worth.

In the days when his credit record was a piece of paper, when he could be elected city solicitor with multiple felonies still on his record (true), the father I never met became concerned with cleaning up his abysmal credit rating. This was a man who traded a one-year-old Plymouth for a brand new Oldsmobile Delta 88 on a small-town government salary with two kids at home and two more by his ex-wife in Atlanta, growing up fatherless.

But his credit was in the crapper. So the story goes he cooked up a little scheme to wipe the slate clean. As the tale goes, he seduced the bank secretary on her lunch break for a quickie at the no-tell motel, then snuck back over to her office at the bank, pulled his paper credit report out of her filing cabinet, and trashed it. I can see each element of this plot so clearly—the seduction, climax, and denouement—that I can hear the sound of the metal drawer in the filing cabinet closing.

This story has legs because it fits with his pattern—the man was a compulsive cheat. Once upon a time, a strange woman kept calling my mother to complain bitterly that my father had gotten this woman pregnant and walked away. Makes sense. My father had repeatedly walked away from his own wives' children. He walked away from two boys by his first marriage. He ran away from me. And he abandoned my brother and sister, repeatedly. Why wouldn't this new little bastard also be his? My mother didn't dispute it. She just asked this poor woman, "What do you expect me to do about it?" If she could have controlled him, she would have.

My father also loved to spend money on himself with only wishful thinking to pay the debt. No sooner than the sheriff wheeled his body out of the Holiday Inn where he'd holed up for the longest weekend, the bank sent a repo man to tow away the car he couldn't afford. My mother insists they weren't even behind on the payments. Odd how grief seizes on small indignities. He told her he had life insurance. He had none.

So even though I never laid eyes on the man, nor he on me, I judged him, blamed him, and executed the sentence of resentment.

So it is I who remained shackled to him, judge and inmate doing time together. Except he broke free. And I remained tethered. How is that? I want to forgive my mother, who is here, so we both can live in peace. Yet I clung to harsh judgment of my father and remained imprisoned by it. Why? Why not let go?

I was asked this rude "why" question by a lovely young Australian journalist named Holly Williams, in a spacious room at a house named for the "father of journalism," Walter Lippmann. Holly worked for the British channel Sky News before joining the American network CBS and becoming a contributor to the legendary news magazine *60 Minutes*. She listened to my long tale of woe and thought I was rather hard on my father.

By tradition, we Nieman Fellows each took one night of the year to host the rest of the class, plus partners and guests, for drinks followed by our own story and the dinner of our choosing. I spent months thinking about my story. I had a slide deck. I waxed on for forty-five minutes or so. Now I fielded questions. Hurry up, I thought. There was Kings' barbecue hot in the lobby, drop-shipped in a Styrofoam cooler from eastern North Carolina to the FedEx in Harvard Square, then reheated in the kitchen at Lippmann House.

I wasn't sure my story would hold up under questioning. Holly's question was simple: "Why are you so angry with him?" It was the kind of question a friend asks a friend. That or a therapist.

Why was I so angry? There was more to her setup. She walked me through it. This won't be verbatim, but I think it captures her premise: "You suffer from alcoholism, right? And your father was an alcoholic? Same. And he died of the disorder, disease, ever what you call it. OK? And you never even met him? So why are you so angry with him?"

"I'm not angry," thought this angry man. "Do I come off as angry?" Well, yes. Evidently. Holly picked up on it, but so had the room. I can tell another person's story in an afternoon. I'll take years telling my own and never see myself clearly. That's why I need others. I can't understand myself without them.

I couldn't answer the "why" question in that moment because I didn't know. With some years to work it out, I think it's because I took it personally. Among recovering codependents, there's a cute acronym—QTIP. Quit taking it personally. My father just did what he did. He didn't do it *to* me.

Then there's my part, my own character defects, which cause me to cling to my sob story. Truth be told, I like blaming him. It's a way of making me look better. I want people to see me and say, "Here's a good dad with his one wife and his four kids, no fatherless boys wandering through life working out their issues. He's in long-term recovery. He's at Harvard." Well la-dee-fucking-dah. Aren't I just man of the year?

I need to let my father go. I need to do it for my own sake. I need to accord him the same compassion I would offer that towheaded baby jerked into foster care on day one. I need to identify with him, flesh of my flesh, the sins of the father visited upon the son.

If I really believe that I am sober through unmerited grace, and not because I beat addiction all by myself, then how can I blame my father? I could be him. No, I am him. I need to identify, not compare. He drank. He dallied. He self-destructed. I drank. I dallied. I self-destructed. Death just got to him quicker.

Years after confronting me that evening, Holly flew from Istanbul to New York when she won the DuPont-Columbia silver baton for the CBS coverage of Syrian refugees. I hired a camera crew and met her on a bench by Riverside Park at dawn. I wanted to document our conversation. She was gracious and generous. When I recalled her "why" question, she hung her head. Said she was embarrassed at her impertinence as a younger reporter. I thanked her for her question. It made me think. Then it made me shift.

We walked to a diner on the Upper West Side. She bought breakfast.

WATCH, LISTEN, AND LEARN

To hear Holly tell her version of this story, visit ManListening.com to view a video clip.

My mom: Nell Martin Watson.
Longwood Gardens. Kennett Square,
Pennsylvania. February 2008.

SHE TRUSTED ME

. . . .

"Is it a sin to want to die?"

Nell Martin Watson
Mom
Morningside assisted living
Albany, Georgia
Summer 2011

On Dying

"Come home, son."

Mom's voice was shaky, needy, heartbreaking. Here I was up at Harvard, having the time of my life, happier than a pig in slop. And she was asking me to fly to Albany, Georgia. Best to just fly to ATL and rent a car. If you could have heard her voice, you would understand. It was the voice of a mother who just needed her son.

She said something about how I had such a calming influence. My parents were still rattling around in that big house, the one they built, the one they'd spent their whole lives as parents in, the one with the apartment on the back for her mother, a three-thousand-square-foot empty nest.

Liz and I were scared to death they would forget a pot on the stove and burn the place down around them. They weren't eating right. They weren't taking their meds right. Their minds weren't right. We bought an elaborate plastic pill case for their many confusing pills. It was labeled Monday through Sunday, color-coded, and sectioned off with times of the day like breakfast and after dinner. But it still depended on them to know what day it was and to load it up, and to remember if they had loaded it, and to actually take it.

I took color photos of each of their pills with a penny next to it, so they could judge size. I hand-labeled the prints and wrote how many to take, put it all on one big card, and laminated the card, so it wouldn't shred. It still didn't work. They needed someone to sort it out, to hand them the pills and the glass of water, someone like a caretaker, like a son. They didn't have a son, not one there anyway. He was off at Harvard having the time of his life while theirs was slipping away.

I knew this would be a problem. I actually went to Dad before taking the fellowship and said straight out that I didn't want to leave them and move way away to Boston at the precise time they needed me. "I hope you win twelve Peabody Awards," he said. Different thing, Dad, but I take your point. I went. But the voicemail from Mom called me back. I felt the old guilt in my gut of a son who has abandoned his Mom in her hour of need.

Dad went on something of a victory lap, his mind fading, but not too far gone for him to appreciate familiar faces. Now was the last chance. I drove them to Atlanta to fly to Philly to drive to Delaware for the American Camellia Society meeting, so he could pick up a lifetime service award. Good thing I was with them. Dad dropped his wallet in the TSA line. Travel drained them. It drained me. He wore a diaper in the hotel room, dressing in front of me. He'd say, "Old age ain't for sissies, son."

Mom came along, same as always, only at least she didn't have to carry box after box of his precious flowers in a vain attempt to win silverware at a camellia show. I have a photo of her, pretty, all did up, makeup on and smiling in the snow at the old DuPont estate.

I took loads of pictures with my Lumix point and shoot, using the photojournalist's trick of watching through the viewfinder to both capture the moment and escape it. Just before the award ceremony, I snapped one. At that moment, he said, "Why are we here?" his face suddenly drained of all expression, my sister's mouth a tense line. When the time came to be gracious and step to the podium and take a plaque in front of a small crowd, he snapped back, for a moment his old self.

There were two more of these public appearances. If you have ever known anyone with Alzheimer's, you know how rare and precious these flickering moments are, before the light goes out. Wait too long, and a public appearance, even at a family reunion, is pointless. A cousin told me of a miracle drug for memory. "There will be no miracles here," was all I could muster.

I flew straight home, skipping Harvard's commencement. Instead I took Dad to First Presbyterian Church (First Prez), where the church had planned to give him another award for teaching Sunday school for fifty-three years. His old law partners showed up. So did the grown-up teens he'd chaperoned in the youth group, PYF, the Presbyterian Youth Fellowship. His original law partner Paul Keenan dropped a hymnal. "Damn," he said, too loud, right there in church. Mom laughed.

I followed Dad to the front of the church to pick up the plaque. The congregation applauded, an unnatural event for staid Presbyterians. I called out, "Dad!" just as he started to return to his seat. He turned back to me. I snapped a picture with his face and the congregation behind him. I took pictures of him hugging the girls and shaking hands with the guys. I took photos of him going out the church door, of him at the luncheon in his honor, of the lighted "ON THE AIR" sign from him teaching Sunday school on WGPC radio. (I was told the call letters stood for World's Greatest Pecan Center.) I printed up the pictures in one of those books you could format on the Mac, with only five copies just for them, and me, and Liz, and his two living sisters. It made Liz cry.

That summer, the kids drove with us from North Carolina to south Georgia to pick up my parents and drive on to Birmingham for his last Watson family reunion. These are small, tame affairs, no alcohol, the Watsons displaying their Church of Christ abstinence. His baby sister, Becky, was in a wheelchair, confused, but she knew him.

Mom freaked out for some reason after the Watson luncheon. She insisted we turn right around and drive another five hours from Alabama back to Georgia, forfeiting the hotel rooms we'd reserved. Her Alzheimer's, coupled with a lifetime of anxiety (she called it "nervousness," and my Dad called it "worrying") made the already long trip that much longer. We got back home well after dark after more than twelve hours in the minivan. "Well," Colleen, my youngest girl, deadpanned, "At least there was ham."

There were no more public appearances for my parents. We took one more trip, the hardest of all, harder than driving the urn with their ashes back home. It was the trip from Morningside assisted living in their hometown where they'd lived their whole lives together to their last assisted living home in a strange land close by us.

It was one of the hottest days of the year. We'd been up late packing. Liz drove her own Toyota truck. Mom's nervous requests, her constant questions, drove Liz crazy. Drove me crazy too. Thank God my daughter Glynis rode with us. For better or worse, Glynis is a lot like me. She inherited a kind of calm manner that seemed to pacify Mom, or at least placate her. We drove across rural Georgia angling toward North Carolina on the two-lane blacktop. The lunch stop at a Hardee's was particularly tough. I hovered. I was afraid they would fall. Breaking a hip is the beginning of the end for many an eighty-something person. It's not the death. It's the dying part. That's where the suffering lies.

By the time the Charlotte skyline came into view, Mom was experiencing something called "sundowners." She was very confused. Why couldn't we just stop? Just stop the car! Just let her out. Just stop right now, son. How much farther? Sweet Jesus, was I this big a whiner?

By then it was after 5 p.m., and the new assisted living place didn't want to admit them after business hours. Let's just bring them in fresh first thing in the morning. No one would be any fresher then, but that wasn't their problem. We got a hotel room. Liz was terrified they would get up and wander. She laid down near the door standing guard all night long. She didn't sleep a wink.

"I want something sweet," Mom said along about 2 a.m.

"Go back to sleep," Liz told her, emphatically.

Mom pleaded like a four-year-old, "There's those little chocolates," she said, thinking of Hershey's minis in the car.

Liz gave in, "Oh, all right, but you're going to sleep after that."

Mothering your mother. A rite of passage. But to us, a strange land.

Once, back home in Albany in her last year of life, we were sitting at the small dining table in the locked Alzheimer's unit called The Gardens. I suppose there was a garden there somewhere. That's where Mom said to me like a bolt from the blue, "Do you think it's a sin to want to die?"

She would not have asked that question of anyone else. My father was not of a mind to answer it. He had his own dementia. No preacher was there visiting, no best friend. She entrusted me and me alone, a son who would understand, a flicker of light on a dark way.

"No, Mom," I said. "It's not a sin."

"'Cause I could just …," she made a small whooshing sound and flipped her hand out palm down like a bird sailing off toward a setting sun.

I could not help my mom become that bird. I could only reassure her that it was the most natural of desires, a universal journey I would someday join her on, and that there was no shame in wanting it.

"

She entrusted me and me alone,
a son who would understand, a
flicker of light on a dark way."

. . . .

Mom taking a bite of cotton candy from my
sister Liz. Tift Park. Albany, Georgia. 1963.

KNOWN, NOT KNOWN

. . . .

"I don't think I ever really knew her."

Liz Watson Fort, my sister
1226 Hilltop Drive
Albany, Georgia
2010 (recounted 2015)

On Secrets

"HAVE YOU SEEN MY BONG?" my sister yelled downstairs.
"THE ONE WITH THE UNICORN ON IT?" She'd hidden it in
the attic behind the chimney. A house full of hardwood furniture,
and Liz was fixated on a unicorn bong. Sentimental value, I guess.
It had been years since she'd even thought of the stupid thing. We
were cleaning out a half century of memories from our parents'
home. There were lots of tears. Three thousand square feet, solid
brick, sitting on an immaculately landscaped three-quarter acre,
the house and land brought $200,000. In a similar neighborhood
in Charlotte, it would have been $800,000. But it was 2010 in
Albany, Georgia, in the throes of the great recession. I called a
lawyer friend of Dad's, who knew the local market. He set me

straight in his south Georgia drawl: "Styoo-urt, the stow-ree of the real estate mah-ket in Awl-benny is that there idn't one."

We sorted through generations of heirlooms and detritus, terrified of not knowing which was which. Everything went one of three places: piled in the living room for the estate sale/donation, on one of the trucks for us, or in a long roll-off dumpster dropped in the half-circle, pea-gravel driveway out front.

We were standing by the dumpster when Liz told me. Our cousin Carol stood beside her and confirmed. Mom's dad had been the town drunk. I swear to God I never knew that. I checked with our cousin Sandy, my best friend John. Yup. They'd all known it too. It was just an article of faith.

What the hell? I'm the reformed drunk in the family. I told Mom that. But she wouldn't tell me about her own father? All of a sudden, by comparing notes with my sister, I understood my mom. Suddenly, her image snapped into focus. She was an eighty-two-year-old little girl, the keeper of secrets. I could hear it clear as a bell. The bedrock commandment of every alcoholic's family: "We don't talk about Daddy's drinking."

My sister and I chafed under Mom's infernal obsession with what other people thought. What would the neighbors say? What would the people at church say? What would the friend at the front door think of your trashy T-shirt, your unmade bed?

"Who gives a shit?" is what we thought. We weren't her. We put it all out there. Love us or hate us, you'd know us. We wouldn't wear a mask of perfection. Mom wouldn't answer the doorbell without makeup.

"I don't think I ever really knew her," my sister told me later, when I debriefed her for a documentary about family. For adopted children, the mother/daughter thing is even more complex. Trust me.

"Do you think she knew herself?" I asked, ever the penetrating journalist. "I don't know," Liz said. My mom had no therapist, no minister, no counselor, confidant, or confessor. She just bottled up all that family shame and stowed it in a padlocked closet deep in her heart. She might as well have told it all herself. Everyone apparently already knew. Besides, some blabbermouth child will eventually spill the beans. My heart hurts for hers.

I feel like this legacy as town drunk is terribly unfair to my granddad. Who wants his whole life to be reduced to a stock character, Otis of Mayberry on *The Andy Griffith Show*? I can assure you more ink has been spilled over that black-and-white punch line of a character than will ever be written of the colorful, multidimensional Edward Boron Martin Jr. of Leesburg, Georgia.

He raised three kids who loved him. He stayed married to the end. He died before I was born. His father, Ed Sr., had been sheriff, a school board member, and a state rep. He'd made the pages of the *Atlanta Journal-Constitution*. Couldn't have been easy being a "junior" to all that. I should know. I'm a junior too.

E. B. Martin Jr. sold heavy equipment, road graders and such. Traveled the state. Didn't stay on the farm full time. Mom said when he'd get sore at my granny, he'd retreat to nurse his wounds at a stump out behind the house. He had a name for this stump. Called it "Old Lonesome."

"What did you think he was doing all those times he went out to 'Old Lonesome?'" my sister laughed at my naiveté. I dunno. Seems obvious looking back. Thinking and drinking. Drinking and thinking.

Alcoholism is the disease of isolation. An alcoholic alone is an alcoholic in trouble. The liquid itself is the distillate of loneliness. I try to describe what it sounds like when the disease speaks directly, when it takes over the human voice, what words it uses. It says, "Go away. I'm fine. Leave me alone." Whether you insist on staying or whether you leave, as long as he drinks, he is alone.

The untreated codependent, the poor family member, my mom, has no numbing agent for the bitter end. They remember the pain because they were fully present to it. They weren't blacked out or passed out. They hold tight to the searing pain. They stuff it down. They bring it out in private moments and play with it.

You can tell your secrets and risk losing your family. Or you can stuff those secrets way down in the dark and cling to the delusion of control. Sooner or later, the secrets control you.

I understand her silence.

WATCH, LISTEN, AND LEARN
To hear Liz tell her own story, visit ManListening.com view a video of Liz Watson Fort.

"

Addiction is the disease of isolation ... when the disease speaks, it says, 'Go away. I'm fine. Leave me alone.'"

. . . .

Annie Pearl and Eddie Rouse.
Albany, Georgia. Circa 2010.

PEARL

. . . .

"No, ma'am. I love you."

Annie Pearl Rouse
1226 Hilltop Drive
Albany, Georgia
Circa 1979

On Race

Seven years after Martin Luther King Jr. was jailed in my hometown for defying our city fathers, Dad sent me to an all-white private school. My dad was one of those city fathers. Didn't they teach me in Sunday school to "honor my father?" I never defied him. I was a middle-aged man before I ever heard the term "seg academy." When I first went to one, I was ten years old.

I went on to take Georgia history in that same segregated academy. But I had to go 400 miles away to college to learn MLK had been arrested three miles from our spacious brick home, just nine minutes by Plymouth station wagon up Pine Avenue past what is now a Krispy Kreme. Everybody in Albany, Georgia, knows the red neon sign "HOT NOW." Just like the weather.

The leading civil-rights figure of our day was arrested across town, while I played in my little wading pool on the grass-covered terrace outside the sliding glass doors of my white bubble, attended by Black women in white starched dresses, white bras, white hose, constricted in whiteness. I'm still reckoning with the weight of that. Dad's long gone, and I never asked him directly about it. I may never know our family's bit part in that historic jailing.

Dad was politically active. He said it was a way to meet people and be of service when he ran for the Georgia House of Representatives before I was born. His old law partner also said that meeting the right people in Atlanta didn't hurt their business when they formed Home Federal Savings and Loan. Dad served two terms in the gold-domed state house and then came home.

But the year Rev. King knelt on the sidewalk and prayed for peace and justice on Pine Avenue, I was a toddler, and Dad was the executive committee chairman of the Dougherty County Democratic Party. His army buddy Asa Kelley was a white mayor in the deep South with a big ole PR problem. Dad's state house pal B. C. Gardner secretly posted a cash bond to spring Dr. King and Ralph David Abernathy from jail, although MLK wanted to remain locked up in protest. "Jail, not bail!" the picketers chanted. The white city fathers looked like the cat that swallowed the canary. King's "Albany Movement" momentarily lost traction in a fight for newspaper headlines.

"We thought Martin Luther King was a skunk," Dad's big sister blurted out, after I more or less forced her to express an opinion. I was not even asking about Albany. I didn't even bring up Dr. King. I was asking her about the fire bomb, the one on the Freedom Riders' bus outside Anniston, Alabama, Dad's hometown.

"Mammy loved us," my aunt persisted, apropos of nothing I could see, again bringing up people who had no connection to the fire bomb or to MLK. "She raised us." "Mammy" in this case was Mattie Cobb, the daughter of slaves, part Cherokee. She is the lone Black face in Watson family photo albums, my white dad pictured as a small boy with big ears standing at her skirt. When Dad's mother died, my granddad prevailed on Ms. Cobb to move into the home at 902 Quintard in Anniston to raise the kids. She had the authority to whip them when they acted out and cuddle them when they were cold. On Sundays, Ms. Cobb would put on petticoats that swished and borrow some of my grandmother's perfume for church.

The day of the Anniston bus bombing, some of the Klan mob came straight from church, still wearing their Sunday finest. Not Mattie Cobb's church. The white folk who slashed the Trailways' tires and chased the limping bus along had just sung hymns and heard Jesus's words from the same King James Bible Black folk used in the churches across town. It was Mother's Day, 1961. Dad had left town more than two decades before. Once they'd forced the bus off the road, a man named "Goober" lit a bundle of rags on fire and threw them through a broken bus window. It exploded. Black smoke roiled. The mob then blocked the door, some shouting, "Burn 'em alive!"

A white trooper fired his gun in the air. The mob paused, not before beating several Freedom Riders bloody. A twelve-year-old white neighbor girl named Janie Miller brought the rs fresh water. Didn't Jesus say something about a

is from an NPR story about the historic event.
I wasn't there. I don't know. But my own story makes no sense
without understanding the time and place. You have to know
where my dad and his people come from. My story is about two
women—Mom and Annie Pearl Rouse.

Not long after I left home, Mom hired Pearl as a once-a-
week maid to cook and clean. Pearl had already raised five kids
of her own. Her husband, Eddie, worked a full-time job at a
manufacturing plant making cardboard boxes. Plus he did a whole
bunch of side work as a "yardman," which people in some parts
would call a "landscaper."

Pearl was helping Eddie cut our grass, trim the hedges, and pick
up flower petals from Dad's camellia bushes when Mom asked her
if she'd like to work inside.

To start, Mom followed Pearl from room to room chatting
away while Pearl tried to get her work done. This might have been
because Mom suspected Pearl might steal the silverware, or because
Mom was pretty picky about how the cleaning got done, or just
because she liked Pearl's company. But all the hovering and chatter
got on Pearl's nerves.

"Miz Watson, you've gotta leave me be if I'm ever gonna get any
work done," Pearl finally confronted my mom. Mom withdrew,
not like the mob, but still.

Mom liked Pearl's work. She grew to like Pearl. Pearl came once
a week or so for more than thirty years. Then Mom paid her to
come to Morningside assisted living with her, to kind of babysit
them, because she liked Pearl's company.

Dad wouldn't accept help from any woman to shower until Pearl stepped in. She said, "Mr. Watson, you ain't got nuthin' I hadn't seen before." He relented. It wasn't easy.

But back to early on, and the getting on of the nerves. Mom went back to Pearl in the early days and said point blank, "You don't like me, do you Pearl?"

"No, ma'am," Pearl said. "I love you."

Pearl was a church going woman. Told me once how God spared their church from a tornado, a tree laid over right up to the church steps but no more. Me, I don't go to church. I go to church basements. And I'm not sure I'd know Jesus if he was wearing his high school name tag. But I thought I heard a little Jesus in Pearl that day. The commandment said, "Love one another." It didn't say anything about liking you.

Pearl and Eddie were the only people named in Mom's last will and testament who were not immediate family. Mom left them each $500. They told me they were thrilled. It's not exactly hitting the Powerball, nothing close to reparations, but they weren't expecting anything.

Following the imperative to "love one another" does not mean just saying "I love you" to people you don't like. Pearl cared for my mother for much of her life. And Mom thought of Pearl to the end.

WATCH, LISTEN, AND LEARN

To hear Pearl tell her own story, visit ManListening.com to view a video of Annie Pearl Rouse.

My oldest daughter, Erin Jivoff Watson,
and me. Photo booth. Logan Square.
Chicago, Illinois.

NOT MINE TO GIVE

. . . .

"The patriarchy oppresses us all, Dad."

Erin Jivoff Watson, my daughter
Kitchen Chicago
Chicago, Illinois
November 2014

On Patriarchy

When it came time for the father of the bride to give a wedding
toast, I moved to the front of the room with a fluted glass of
ginger ale. Everyone else had champagne. I prepared nothing, no
three-by-five card with notes, jokes, tears. I winged it.

The dumbest thing popped into my head. A memory of me
dragging my two little girls to the men's room at Brown's Diner
on the corner of Blair and 21st in Nashville. Brown's grilled
a great, greasy cheeseburger. The girls liked it well enough.
More importantly for my purposes, the diner delivered cold
beers promptly and plenty of 'em, the better to ease Daddy's
throbbing head.

I loved taking the girls to the Dragon Park. That's the
nearby playground with a giant mosaic tile dragon arcing

out of the Tennessee earth for the girls to climb. Plus it was a hop, skip, and a jump out from Natchez Trace and close to the all-important Brown's.

I did not love taking two little girls to the men's room at Brown's. I'd find a stall, usher both of them inside, latch the door, and use both hands to hold one or the other over the toilet to keep them from falling in. The stall walls were covered floor to ceiling with graffiti, occasionally witty but mostly just crude.

Erin scanned up one wall and down the other while her little sister Glynis looked on. That's when my bright, eldest daughter began to read aloud: "There was a young lad from Nantucket ...." Something like that. It's hard holding your daughter over the disgusting seat with one hand while covering her eyes with the other, trying to shield them from every scrawled symbol fraught with meaning.

As I told the story while toasting her at her wedding, I reimagined my response as a warped, slow motion "NOOOOOOOOOOO." I wrapped up my bridal toast with a conclusion: "And that's what made Erin a poet."

As I now reimagine the reaction of my daughter's wedding party to this little tale, I'd say it was mixed. Her Aunt Kathy looked confused, maybe seeing it as a missed opportunity? Some of Erin's friends laughed politely. Erin saw it as one more dad joke.

"That's m'dad."

My toast was no more unorthodox than the science fiction read aloud from a paperback during the wedding. We had spent the previous afternoon decorating the hall, a cavernous brick warehouse with windows flooding daylight, the wedding planned precisely at sunset. It was beautiful. Gotta hand it to 'em. My daughter was beautiful, dressed in mermaid blue worthy of a sea dragon, bathed in the golden hour.

We walked through the ceremony several times the day before. She told us where to stand. She told her sister when to sing. She told me what to say—nothing. I'd heard these instructions before. "Your job? Close mouth. Sign check. Think you can handle it?"

I signed the check. It was half what I thought about giving them until Lorraine reminded me I might soon need to match it for another couple of daughters. I had a problem with the closing mouth part. I thought I was entitled to tease Erin. "When is the part where I walk you down the aisle and give you away?"

That's when she said it: "The patriarchy oppresses us all, Dad." I had no idea what that meant. Years later, I'm still not exactly sure. But it was pretty clear there would be no giving away of this bride.

We pulled it off. She pulled it off. The last-minute nerves were crushing, a heart attack waiting to happen. But just after the ceremony, amidst all the details that crowded my daughter's brain, came a lone waiter making a beeline straight for me, fluted glass in hand. It was ginger ale, just for me. My daughter is an incredibly thoughtful person.

She does not belong to me. She does not belong to her brilliant husband, NickD. She belongs only to herself. That I would think otherwise is oppressive, and not just to her.

WATCH, LISTEN, AND LEARN
To hear Erin talk to her dad, visit
ManListening.com to view the video.

Xuddur, Somalia. December 1992. Photo
courtesy of Fred Clarke, *Nashville Banner*.

SHE FIRED ME

. . . .

"These things are never easy."
Deborah, boss
WCNC-TV
Charlotte, North Carolina
January 9, 2015

On Fear

She seemed afraid of me. I should have been afraid of her, but she
seemed afraid of me. She had the power to fire me, and she did.
She had the man behind her. To me, she was the man. What power
did I have? Did she think I was going to snap and lash out? Had
I ever shown any indication of violence against anyone—let alone
a woman, let alone a boss? What threat did I represent to her? It
took me years to even consider the possibility that *SHE* was afraid
of *ME*.

For people in fear, a job in local TV news is like a drunk
tending bar. There's always fuel for the flame. My buddy Jelly put
it best: "Whatever category the hurricane is at sea, in the middle of
the newsroom, it's always a Cat 5."

Local TV news is nonstop awfulizing. I spent thirty-two years in it. It's harmful enough just passively humming away in the corner of the pancake house, a constant nagging crawl on repeat. Working in the biz concentrated my exposure to the toxins. For decades I was immersed in it, distilled frame by frame on an incessant loop. I didn't know any other way.

So it's taken this old newsman a long time to see she was just afraid. I was afraid. We were all afraid. We all swam in a fishbowl of fear, constantly on the lookout for something new to be afraid of, and never realizing that we were in the water because we made the water. We made the water, and the bowl, and the bright blue gravel, and the helmeted diver blowing bubbles from the bottom.

We brought the fear. We manufactured it. We packaged it. We commoditized it. We monetized it. It was the product and the service. The goods. We marketed, advertised, and sold it. And we profited from it. Then we bought it and repackaged it and repurposed it and sold it again. And again. And again.

We researched fear. We consulted fear. We social marketed FOMO, fear of missing out.

Why?

Because it's reliable. If you're playing the short game, fighting death more than living life, fear is a safe bet. Guaranteed ROI. 24/7 demand. We're all gonna be there someday, no matter how faithful or how Zen, begging for our mommies just moments before the white light, clinging to the shit-stained sheets, never imagining a floating painless realm of bliss.

So we die a thousand times each day at noon, 6, and 11, as we bring death a thousand times into a thousand homes, multiplying it—not just any deaths but only the most despicable, the most violent. Swim in that for weeks, months, years. Then tell me why you would not be afraid of your hotshot investigative reporter on the chopping block, this man who has raised four kids on direct deposit from the fear industrial complex, now himself, the hitman, your target.

News is toxic, corrosive, and ultimately unhealthy. Prolonged exposure should come with a Surgeon General's black box warning. We're only beginning to discover the links between news consumption and the twin epidemics of anxiety and depression. I live a much happier life without producing it.

As I type these words sitting in bed at 3:03 a.m., I have a spreadsheet tab open showing a few dozen journalism award entries for a $20,000 prize. Only one can win. Good thing I'm just one judge. I can choose between children sodomized, or immigrants tortured, or cancer in our water. As a palate cleanser, maybe there's just a good old-fashioned pol cheating on his wife. These are the best in our business, the best of the best, Pulitzer entries cut and pasted into another contest. The writing is riveting, compelling. They're hard to read back to back. I need to take a walk, breathe fresh air, see the crocuses coming up, the forsythia's yellow-green buds.

When the boss called me into her office to say, "You really need to up your game," which I saw as a transparent setup job some months before my firing, she brought in the HR manager as silent witness, a tipoff to me if ever there was one. I did not understand the game. I did not know we were playing a game. I got in my car and drove to the office of a good attorney. I needed to understand the rules. I did not trust her to keep score.

When she finally brought the hatchet down one Friday afternoon, she assembled an audience in her spacious office—my new supervisor, a few others, a burly guy with his arms folded standing behind me. And to what end? I'm really not sure. To wrestle me to the ground? Did they take some pleasure in it? I began to take notes, reporter to the end, my handwriting shaky. I can only make out the one quote: "These things are never easy."

"

We're only beginning to discover the links between news consumption and the twin epidemics of anxiety and depression."

....

Jack Watson and Zuzu the westie. Kia
Rondo. Charlotte, North Carolina.

IRRELEVANT

. . . .

"You are irrelevant."

Facebook troll
Charlotte, North Carolina
January 10, 2015

On Contempt

Her Facebook profile said she worked for a big hospital and went
to Elevation Church. So maybe I had it coming. I had taken
a whack or two at its founding preacher and resident idol, a
multimillion-dollar raconteur who created an onstage persona as
"Pastor Steven." In my experience you meet better Christians in the
county lockup.

I had just gotten fired from a TV group that once (in a prior
incarnation) flew our investigative team to the shareholders
meeting in Dallas and called us up front with the CEO to put
our picture in the annual report. Now I got the we-wish-him-
well email one Friday afternoon. Well, I didn't get it. The rest of
the staff got it. By then they'd locked me out of my email and
confiscated my ID.

That's when the troll struck on Facebook. Why, oh why do I spend a millisecond on the trolls? They will suck the life out of you. Stop it, Stuart. Just stop it. But like Lot's wife, Mrs. Lot, I look back. And as I look back, I'm frozen into a statue of salt. No wonder my kids call me "salty."

"Sit down, Mr. Watson. You are irrelevant," the troll wrote. Why do I care? Well I think it stuck with me because in my heart I believed it.

I had investigated Steven Furtick, "Pastor Steven," the charismatic, Joel Osteen hugging, *New York Times* bestselling televangelist who was Elevation Church. I caused him and thousands of his followers offense by asking a super simple question that I've *still* never really heard answered: where does all the money come from, and how much of it goes to Pastor Steven?

Safe to say, it's a metric shit ton of money, give or take. I'll just put it this way: he built himself a mansion just short of heaven with seven and a half baths, because you never know when company's gonna stop by. I won't start on the clothes, the hair, the personal security guard posse. You know, like Jesus would do.

What possible business is this of mine? Well, I pay taxes. And megachurch televangelists are entitled (thank you, Congress) to something called the "parsonage allowance" for their humble 16,000-square-foot homes. It just means their monthly mortgage is a tax-free perk of the preacher man. I commit the blasphemy of asking what his flock will not—how much?

My pesky question caused a momentary kerfuffle in our little backwater and evidently generated a resentment on the part of my Facebook troll. I guess she thought the Christ-like thing would be to kick a man when he'd just been fired. How elevating.

Me? I sat at the head of my family dinner table and cracked wise about killing myself. Not to worry, I told my assembled wife and kids. Like George Bailey's worst fears in *It's a Wonderful Life,* I was worth more to them dead than alive. They could cash in my 401(k), the equity in our mere 2,500 square feet, and of course, a half million or so in life insurance. How's that for being relevant?

"I've got good news and bad news," said my buddy John who sold me the half-mil policy.

"What's that?" I asked.

"The good news is that the policy will cover you if you off yourself," he reassured me, somewhat.

"The bad news is that you're underinsured," he explained. Actuarially speaking, Lorraine would live another thirty-odd years. She'd run out of money.

"And," he added, "She'll spend every day cursing your name for doing this to her."

Shit. Might as well live. Why give little Stevie and his minions the satisfaction?

Smartassery aside, I had nightmares about work for four years. None of them involved getting fired. I was always back at work on deadline, the second hand ticking toward the six o'clock news. I was writing. No one was editing. Nothing was getting done. Plus no one else seemed to remember I'd been fired.

"Guys, I can't be in the building," I'd insist. "I don't belong here. Security's gonna come get me."

No one else in the dream seemed concerned. "Just get it done," they'd say. But it wasn't getting done. I was a fraud. The ten Emmys? The three Peabody Awards? The Harvard fellowship?

The thirty-two years in the biz? None of it meant anything. I'd fooled a lot of people for a long time. I was a big, fat poser.

"I don't belong here." That is a familiar feeling, the oldest of feelings. I'm not legit. Legitimate is being part of. It's belonging. I feel in my core I am not a part of. I do not belong. This place is not my home. I could not build a home, whatever the size, that would make me feel at home. In my Father's house are many mansions, but down here, I'm not at home.

Feeling cut off and apart from is at once profoundly disturbing and completely familiar. Why am I reading the Facebook troll? Why do I collect the troll comments and roll them around like worry beads so that I feel like a total piece of shit? Because I need the shame spiral like a drunk needs a drink. I may be blubbering into my beer, but at least I was right. I told you I was worthless. Self-pity bought me a lot of beer.

As long as I'm being honest, the thought that really kept me from buying shells to load my shotgun was Jack. My only son was going to college. He didn't need his only dad blowing his head off. It would fuck him up. I very much did not want that. In my darkest hours, when I didn't really care about me, I did care about Jack.

Why is it that if you call me a piece of shit I'll basically nod in agreement, but if you say I'm a good dad, I can't accept it? One thing is just a bedrock fact—I raised a decent son. I raised him up. You might even say I elevated him.

The word "relevant" comes from the medieval Latin *relevare* meaning to raise up. Irrelevant equals "putdown." You can't elevate by putting down. Someone said faith without works is dead. Who said that? I dunno. Might have been Pastor Steven.

From the dim recesses of Sunday school memories, I recall my own version of a Bible verse. Google tells me it's Proverbs 22:6. My version? Raise up a son in the way he should go, and when he's grown, he'll do just fine.

Jack is upstairs asleep. This year he graduates. Now he's lifting me.

Jack (LOUD) and Erin (quiet) at Erin's
graduation day brunch. Carrboro,
North Carolina. May 2007.

LOUD AND QUIET

. . . .

"It's a lot quieter."

Ex-colleague
WCNC-TV
Charlotte, North Carolina
January 2015

On Accountability

My boss called me a "pompous ass." I laughed. He was right.

I tend to dominate the conversation. Any conversation. I talk over people. I have a big voice. Really loud, like shouting. This can be good if you need someone to suddenly stop a room to say, "CALL 9-1-1!" or, "IS THERE A DOCTOR HERE? THIS MAN HAS COLLAPSED." Both of which I have done. But day in, day out, my big voice is a pain. It hurts.

Just ask anyone who had to sit within fifty feet of me, especially when I'm on the phone. It's like I'm oblivious. More than a few of my colleagues complained about it at work, even people who liked me. I mean Jeremy had to sit right next to me. Allison, just a couple of desks up, Hollywood Squares style. Rachel, right beside me in those god-awful half cubicles with the walls lowered below ear-level, five feet away, with no barrier. The newsroom was basically a boiler-room situation. There's no escaping the blast.

For months, years, my coworkers endured my weekly rants. Phone slamming. F-bombs. They complained. I ignored them. They tried to ask nicely. I made it a joke. I was getting older. I was hard of hearing. Plus I ignored them. I was becoming my father. I was getting even less self-aware. I just never stopped.

Then one day they fired me. The new boss did. It wasn't just the yelling. They basically needed to shove a lot of people out the door to save money. But my yelling didn't help. I sued them. Eventually we settled. "Did you win?" people asked. "We settled," I said. That means no. No, I did not win. I got a little money, and I'll never work for their big company or any like it again, which is mainly a good thing. Still, health insurance for me and the Mrs. would have been nice. I'm sixty now.

I thought they'd miss me. I got a few calls. Some people never spoke to me again. Jeremy and Allison and Rachel did. We remained friends. But they never forgot the yelling. One woman, who I thought was my friend, just said, "It's a lot quieter now." I was hurt.

It took me about five years to get it through my thick head. They liked me well enough. Most did anyway. They just didn't like all the noise.

I've tried to get better. I don't know if I have. My wife, sometimes my kids, still say, "Lower your voice. You're yelling."

I'll never work in one of those cubicle situations again. It's not good for me. And it's really not good for those poor souls who had to work around me.

I have my own tiny shop now. I work out of a common area in a coworking space. People smile at me and say hi when I buzz in. No one complains. I try to be a decent neighbor. I work around many artists, painters, weavers, and such. I tap away at my laptop. I put in earbuds to screen audio. I listen to ambient music on Spotify.

When I take a phone call, I try to step outside, even in the cold. It just seems to work better that way, my big laugh drifting down the street.

Me as superhero wannabe, "FixerMan."
Illustration by Callie Catchpole.

RIDING WITH THE PART-TIME STRIPPER TO THE METHADONE CLINIC

. . . .

Friend
Charlotte, North Carolina
Circa 2015

On Codependency

I judged her. Of course I judged her.

I judged her tattoos. I judged her clothes. I judged her lack of clothes.

And I was completely wrong.

She didn't talk much in large groups. I judged what she didn't say. I filled in the blanks. I made up stories. None of the stories involved me. She seemed overtly sexual. I am a big, fat dork. No good came from the dork approaching the sexy girl. Do you not remember fifth grade?

After some months of meetings, I happened to hold her hand during the Lord's Prayer. Don't get carried away. It was kinda clammy. She said hey. Gradually we began talking.

The more I found out, the more she became just another sufferer, and even more mystical. She had a kid. The father died in a single-vehicle wreck, probably loaded. She didn't want to know. She never got over it. He had several what she called "baby mamas." She got along with the others OK.

She had become a mother about the age I lost my virginity but a generation later. As repressed as I was, that's how free she was. She had a mouth on her. And full lips with that mouth. I became fixated on her.

I'm kind of a button-downed married guy, missionary position, twice a week tops. I took her for a freaky, unmarried girl, up for anything at anytime. I am well aware what this sounds like. In the textbooks, it's described as "boy meets girl on AA campus." In the rooms, it's called "thirteenth stepping" when gray-haired men target fresh, young women. Let's just say it's frowned upon. There are unspoken rules. Then there were the messy lives of the men who passed along those rules, rules for other people.

There are cutesy phrases: "two sickies don't make one wellie" and "you can't start a car with two dead batteries." There's the misogyny that dates back to the room full of old, white men in Akron: "under every skirt there's a slip."

I made up my own rules. I never went to a strip club with her. I never caught her act. She could talk about sex. I did my best never to bring it up or comment on her sex talk, which was considerable. I became practiced at the Christian side hug. She once asked me to sponsor her in twelve-step recovery. Not no, but hell no!

Then something clicked. We became friends. Close friends. She gave me a little sign from a gift shop that said, "We'll always be best friends ... because you know too much."

But it wasn't healthy. She went to see Ghostface Killah and drank too much expensive Grey Goose and puked all night. I lectured her. She'd hang up or walk off. She said heroin was the problem, not weed or booze. She'd been on methadone for years, never finding the off ramp. She smoked weed when she could avoid a piss test.

But she'd occasionally talk about freelancing with "zannies" or Xanax. I told her benzos plus opioids equals dead. "You don't want your son growing up an orphan." I sounded paternal, naggy. "Please tell me you're not gonna do that. Promise me." I was way too involved. I couldn't even see it.

She once told me she could make $600 in a lunch shift stripping. Or she might make $60. Her boyfriend didn't like it. I didn't jump in the middle of that. I just didn't understand why she tried to sell Mary Kay or hold down some little temp job if she was really that good of a stripper. I bought some bronzer or skin toner from her, glorified aftershave. It was all right. I don't dunk on Mary Kay.

One day I rode with her to the clinic so she could pick up her methadone. She rolled down the windows and lit up a cigarette, the long, slow kill. She said she wanted a boob job, but she didn't have the money. This also mystified me. What was so wrong with her boobs?

They call the methadone dispensary a "treatment center." I'm not sure what they're treating. It's like treating drunks with near beer. I get that you can die from alcohol withdrawal without medical detox. But this medical treatment is unending. I don't get it. Probably comes from heroin and oxys never being my thing.

What exactly was going on here? If I were straight-up fucking her, that wouldn't be great, but it would at least be understandable. Old man. Pretty young thing. Gossipers probably assumed as much already. If it were a school-boy crush, it was a highly dysfunctional one. It took me some time to get even a little clarity on what was going on in my head.

More than I wanted to fuck her, I wanted to fix her fuckedupedness. I'm a fixer. I'm a wannabe healer. I think I'm Superman, but I'm not even Clark Kent. I'm more Mr. White, crotchety editor at the *Daily Planet*, nagging voice of reason. I wanted to rescue her, to save her, but she didn't want saving.

I don't see her much anymore. She's still with the boyfriend. Last I heard she had another kid. She doesn't strip any more or sell Mary Kay. That was a phase. It's unfair of me to stick a label on her based on a phase. You could just as easily label me: enabler, codependent, needy, pathetic.

She drove me into other rooms, other groups, groups of other recovering fixers, out there trying to control their own wild, broken, chaotic friends and family. In rooms of recovering addicts, there's a lot more laughter. In rooms of recovering families, there's a lot more tears. My old mentor said both were necessary, called 'em "the sound effects of recovery."

"

I wanted to rescue her, to save her, but she didn't want saving."

. . . .

Illustration by Al Bigley, based on a selfie
and my flawed memory. Lake Norman,
North Carolina.

WANTING AND GETTING

. . . .

"What do men want?"

Friend
Lake Norman, North Carolina
Circa 2015

On Desire

She shows me a cell phone pic of her ass in a thong. Pretty sure
Miss Manners doesn't have one rule for this, but I don't have time
to check. She hands me her phone. The pic is on the phone. I don't
know who took it, but I'm being asked for some type of response.

I'm in my mid-fifties. She's in her mid-thirties. We're friends,
very good friends, but that's it. She's beautiful, but I do not have
a crush on her, let alone one of my obsessions. I'm long-married.
She's never-married, just thinking about dating a new guy she is
iffy about. The old one, the one who was not leaving his wife no
matter how much he said he would, is gone.

I have been sleeping with my wife longer than she has been
alive. She is three years older than my oldest daughter, six years
older than my middle daughter, a dozen years older than my
youngest daughter. I tell her these things. To be honest, I am

flattered this young woman trusts me. I am not going to abuse this privilege.

She could have been saying a great many things. She could have been just fishing for a compliment, wanting affirmation that she's hot. She could have been asking, "'Would you hit that?" I honestly don't think so. There's a lot more context obviously. But the context is all mine. I bring it.

We are of different generations. So I have no idea what she was saying. I only know what I heard, which is not what she said out loud. I heard, "I'm insecure. I'm tired of years spent auditioning for Mr. Right and getting Mr. Not Just Yet or Mr. Not Again or Mr. ManBoy, either not ready for adulting or tired of it. I don't have time for this shit. I'd like children. So I'd like some straight up information from a man I actually trust." Maybe she was asking *IF* she could trust a man, stepping onto the ice, half expecting to fall through.

"Can I ask you something?" she said sometime later. I was giving her a lift, dropping her off somewhere. "What do men want?"

I stifled a lot of smart-ass answers and tried to act like a grown-up. "Depends a great deal on the man and when you catch him." That's a kind of sober answer. Not sure how helpful it was.

Look, I'm sure my motives were not entirely pure, and if I took one drink, let alone a dozen shots, I'm certain I would embarrass myself, old limp-dick drunk that I am, long on talk and short on performance. There's a good chance I would not even remember what I said or did, subject to blackouts as much as impotence. There's a thousand ways that could end even worse.

I know my therapists—all of them women—plus my sponsor, plus my wife, plus my buddies would unanimously judge this to be a terrible idea, putting myself in a car with this young woman. I know because I've asked them all. And you know what? It's not up to them.

I didn't hit on this woman. I am not a grabber. I am not a creep. I ask myself if this woman were wasting away in a coma, skeletal, unrecognizable, the face of death, would I visit her hospital bed, stand over her, say a prayer, say goodbye? I think so. I've done it for others.

I saw her years later for coffee. We catch up from time to time. She was late, selling her furniture, looking for a roommate. She had broken up with some young hunk. He'd been flirting with another girl from back home, not having sex with that girl yet, but she could spot the signs. It was time.

I was pleased we had remained friends. I was proud I had remained married. I am proud I work on my marriage.

"Never confuse intimacy with 100 percent disclosure," my friend Tim's therapist tells him. That's good stuff, I said. I'm totally stealing that. "Could save you a lot of money," he laughs.

ManListening episode with my former
colleague, Colleen Odegaard of
NBC Charlotte and *Wake Up To
Your Life* podcast. Photo courtesy of
Mariano Archdeacon.

MOTIVATION

. . . .

"Sweetheart, you are not an empathic listener."

Lorraine Jivoff
Wife
Captiva Island, Florida
Spring 2017

On Empathy

I was working with Alix Felsing as a developmental editor when
she suggested I take a personality test called the DISC assessment.
Said it might help me organize my thoughts.

Fun fact: the DISC questionnaire was created by the same man
who brought us Wonder Woman. The superhero was based on his
and his wife's polyamorous partner. Makes me wonder about her
DISC scores.

My $60 test and Alix's helpful interpretation (more than $60,
worth every penny) said I was an "empathic listener." I became
somewhat puffed-up at this phrase. I decided to share it with my
wife. You know, as proof of what a sensitive, tuned-in kind of a guy
I am. After all, the computer said so.

Lorraine is my one true love. We met in college and have been together ever since. We have four grown kids together. We have never had a polyamorous partner. At this point, it's tough enough just being amorous partners. Having Polly around would just be exhausting.

We were taking a family vacation, all renting a big house together on the Florida gulf coast when I broke the news to her. "Honey, you'll never guess what this test revealed about your husband. Says right here, I …" (dramatic pause) "… am an empathic listener."

We had left the house and were walking past the sea grapes down to the beach. She was wearing her sun visor and her cover-up over her one-piece swimsuit. I glanced over for her reaction.

"Sweetheart," she said. "You are *not* an empathic listener."

Gotta be honest. That stung a little.

Upon further reflection I determined that at least one of three things was true:

A. The test was right. I'm a swell listener. And I get no respect at home.

B. I managed to bullshit the test. I'm really not a good listener. And Lorraine was right.

C. I listen to everyone except the woman I love.

I'm thinking it's C. Or possibly D, all of the above.

But that got me wondering about a kind of protracted experiment. I'd prevail on female friends and family to record conversations with me. I'd tote my indestructible Marantz digital audio recorder around the country like the love child of Studs

Terkel and Alan Lomax, engaging women I knew in conversation. That way, Lorraine could listen to me listening and hear what a great listener I was. That'd show her.

So I did. Turns out I suck as a listener. Especially to women. It's right there on the tape. Lorraine had always claimed I was dismissive of women. I dismissed her. Woman, please. But now she has evidence.

I interrupted. I interrogated. I dominated. On occasions I argued. I gave advice when no one asked. Don't get me wrong. I had my moments. I've put a lot of that out into the world as the podcast called ManListening®. But some of it is un-friggin-listenable, even to me, and I adore my own voice. Yet it is all—100 percent of it—instructive.

I didn't make it easy on myself. I started with a friend who was in hospice care dying of cancer. I recorded two conversations with Lucy before they upped her meds and she couldn't finish her thoughts. I was aware of how precious those lucid moments were that she allowed me to preserve, and so was she. Within months she would be dead.

Over the course of more than a year, I recorded lots more conversations—a cousin in Houston, a former NFL cheerleader in Tampa, a doctor who survived breast cancer in Nashville, a teen mom in Charlotte who grew up to start a shelter for moms using her retirement funds, a transracial adoptee in Harlem, and dozens of other women. I started off avoiding celebrities and anyone pitching anything. I talked to more than one birth mom who gave up her baby for adoption. For an adult adoptee to listen with all his heart to a birth mom is powerful stuff, even if it's not my own mother.

Some moments were transcendent. But lots of times I felt like I didn't know what the hell I was doing. I often lapsed into interviewing, reverting into playing the TV reporter again. "Stop it!" I told myself. This was different. I was no longer just angling for the sound bite. I wanted to let go of control and see where the conversation would lead.

I tried to practice silence. I failed. I would share my own personal experience when it seemed on point. But I misjudged a lot. Lots of times I drifted off and ignored what was being said. I began to think of myself less as journalist and more as conversationalist. It was messy. It was uncomfortable. It was exhilarating!

For an old broadcast dude fumbling around in a new audio medium, I did a lot of things right. I insisted all conversations be one-on-one and face-to-face. No webcams, no satellite shots, no cell phones. I never once sat in a studio with over-the-ear headphones and big mics covered in black foam windscreens. None of this "lean into that microphone will you sweetheart?" No, no, NO!

I asked my friends if they'd sit in their favorite seat at home, the one even the cat wasn't allowed in. Might be a kitchen stool. Might be an end of the sofa. Might be an easy chair.

I carefully asked my friend Marnae about the loss of her daughter Torie as she sat in a wicker chair on the porch of a dock house at Lake Norman, ski boats blasting by in the background. On a couch at my coworking space, C3 Lab, in the noisy heart of Charlotte's Historic South End, I listened as my friend Gay described her son's deadly heroin overdose. At the kitchen table in her halfway house, I spoke with my friend "Tina," a recovered crack addict, about Child Protective Services taking her daughters.

The result was authentic human conversation, not showbiz celebrity artifice. It was perfect for the relatively new medium of podcasting. We changed some names to preserve anonymity and abbreviated others, but we didn't cut f-bombs. Sorry, Mom. It's just how some of us talk.

Once we were real with each other, and once I shut up for a change, I was totally blown away by the stories I had never heard from some of my closest female friends. We're talking suicide, debilitating depression, abortion—the moments that make us. I never heard because I never listened. I never listened because I never stopped talking about me. So exactly how good a friend could I have been?

The big story that surprised me was of strong women bouncing back. I believe the word of the day is "resilience." Every single woman had some story of deep wounds. Cancer. Divorce. The loss of children. A harrowing amount of sexual assault. This superpower of resilience, of abandoned children growing up to become superheroes, helps others achieve their own miraculous transformation. We can all relate, women and men.

I must confess a sneaky ulterior motive in all this. No, it's not to get laid. I'm not that guy. No, I wanted to kind of make amends. I wanted to create a counterpoint to angry-man talk radio. I've been that guy. Instead I received an audacious vision. I would tell you it came to me in a dream, but you wouldn't believe it. My revelation? "One Voice Can Change The Conversation."

I'm proud of ManListening®. From humble podcast, ManListening® is really a movement, equal parts art form, cathartic healing and ministry. I believe one day it will catch on. I just hope I live to see it! But more important than any of that, Lorraine says I'm a better listener. More empathic. Still not great. But the woman loves me in spite of myself!

WATCH, LISTEN, AND LEARN

To hear Colleen Odegaard and dozens of other women tell their own stories, check out ManListening wherever you get your podcasts.

"

*This superpower of resilience,
of abandoned children growing
up to become superheroes,
helps others achieve their own
miraculous transformation."*

. . . .

Pillow in Lucy Lustig's hospital room.
Novant Health Presbyterian Medical
Center. Charlotte, North Carolina.
Fall 2017

LUCY IN HOSPICE

. . . .

"I don't have time."

Lucy Lustig
Charlotte, North Carolina
September 2017

On Gratitude

"I don't want to scare you," she said, a little self-consciously. Then she screamed in pain. It was god-awful. The woman felt like she had to warn me. But she couldn't really prepare me; I had signed up for this.

Lucy was in hospice care by this point. She had weeks, maybe months left. They put up a hospital bed in the living room of the house her partner, Kenny, had built with his bare hands, installing cabinetry, wiring, and fixtures, everything but the carpet.

I came to record her voice, preserve her story. I was going to practice listening to women, one at a time. To start, I picked a doozie. But Lucy was game. She liked the idea. She thought of it as documentary work, a story all about her. I thought of it as a podcast, all about me. We were both wrong. It was about more than both of us. It was about transcendence.

She talked about the boys at Independence High School calling her a lesbian after glancing at her clothes, her hair. If she'd have fit the bill, she would have owned it. But she wasn't. She talked about meeting Kenny early in her recovery, how laidback he was, how he gave her space to get to her feet. He taught her to ride her own motorcycle. The attraction? "Black leather is black leather." True that.

Not knowing if a conversation will be your last gives the words added weight. Trivia becomes profundity. She watched Japanese anime on TV as a distraction from the pain. It's her pain. She's allowed. I asked her to turn the TV off, to share her pain.

We were both aware the window of time when we could talk was closing. Even so, the conversation rambled. I didn't try to steer it. Not much anyway. She gave me one long set of instructions about a huge stack of old snapshots from yard sales, family candids, and magazines. She wanted them curated and photocopied, blown up and moved around to create a narrative, a piece of art that would survive her. What narrative? Up to us.

She wanted me to carry them to an art class buddy. Go ahead. Get started. We never did. "I'm not an artist," I protested. "And Talking Heads weren't musicians," she said. I heard one friend complain at her memorial, "Lucy never finished anything." And yet we'd just walked out of a service in which two women read poems inspired directly by Lucy. She finished her art through others.

For work, Lucy once managed some apartments on North Tryon in uptown Charlotte. She imagined a film about the crazy mishmash of transient tenants. She'd run an art studio. She believed in food as art, good food, out of the land. She believed it could heal the earth and us at the same time. She wanted me to fetch her a book about it. "We don't have time," I said.

One night sitting at her bedside, I was gossiping about some mutual friend, complaining what a pain in the ass this person could be. I recruited others in the room to pile on. Lucy held up a weak hand, palm out, to bring such talk to a halt. She said, "I don't have time."

When she got to a part of her story about how people close to her had betrayed her, sold her out, and left her empty, she suddenly just let go of the resentment with a quick prayer. "I release you," she said. She would have to let go of all of it soon enough. She knew.

She mourned her death in real time. She'd suddenly cry in wracked sobs for about a minute, then return to conversation. I asked her what artist she felt compelled to see live. She talked about seeing Joni Mitchell. She began singing an iconic melody from *Blue*, trailing off in tears.

In two weeks, the docs upped her meds for anxiety and the pain, and she could no longer complete a thought. Leaving my recorder behind, I kept visiting her at Presbyterian Hospital, then at the nursing home. I saw her skeletal, in diapers, a cross-stitch nearby with a quote about what friendship meant. I brought books to read, my favorites from Dr. Seuss—*Yertle the Turtle* and *Sleep Book*. I never got to read them out loud to her. She was asleep a lot.

She died around Thanksgiving. I've always thought of my recordings as time capsules. I'm grateful to have preserved her voice, more grateful still to share it.

WATCH, LISTEN, AND LEARN

To hear Lucy's full story, visit ManListening.com or wherever you get your podcasts to access the full podcast episode, "Lucy Lustig."

My father, Henry Scott Schmid, Jr.,
shortly before his death of
acute alcoholism.

UNWIRING THE BOMB

. . . .

"Bull. Shit."

Tammy Bell,
Relapse-prevention specialist
Charlotte, North Carolina
Circa 2017

On Self-Pity

I pay women to tell me I'm wrong. It's usually somewhere around $3 a minute with a forty-five-minute minimum. A decent lawyer would be twice that, but my friend Sally Higgins does a little pro bono work to keep me out of serious scrapes. When my wife and daughters found out how much money I spend for women to tell me I'm wrong, they offered to do the job for free. Very funny.

I'm not asking these women to shame me. They're not telling me I'm bad. This isn't dominatrix territory. I'm not a bad boy. I'm an ignorant man. I've had enough of shame. I once spent $800 on a therapist for her shame group. Before it was all over, I felt like she shamed me in front of the whole group. That was therapeutic. I'll never go back, but it's $800 well spent.

To tell me that I'm wrong is easy. I can get that at home. To learn how I'm wrong is worth the money and then some. To learn how to create a tiny pause, just before being wrong yet again is golden. It's worth years of therapy, coaching, counseling. I aspire to make a better class of mistake, to move up a level in the video game.

This isn't about comparing myself to anyone else. One day, one of the church ladies outside a twelve-step meeting tells me she's just so … *proud* of how well "you people" are doing. Us people. You know, the drunks and junkies and sex freaks that use their church basement more than they do. I like to think we look more like Matthew, Mark, Martha, and Mary than they do. Anywho, I felt a teensy bit judged. Then it hit me. If I can make just one person each day feel a little bit morally superior, my work here is done. I'm not trying to get good. I'm trying to get well.

Dad always said, "Do your best." I always heard, "Be perfect, or we'll give you back." Where was "back?" I didn't know. But I got the feeling I didn't want to know. I've spent my whole life desperately wanting to belong. The feeling of terror and emptiness, of falling untethered through space, is wired into me. It's the intersection of two hells—grief and panic. A feeling triggered by shame.

I didn't know what my "best" was. I thought best meant perfect. Anything less than best meant sin, and sin meant the worst of two hells. I lived much of my life in those hells. Vodka salved the burns until it fueled the flames. Don't tell me drugs kill. Alcohol saves lives. Right up until it doesn't.

Shame is just self-loathing. Self-loathing means self-destructing. Vodka takes longer than throwing yourself off a high-rise, but it's just as sure. I'd believe in shame if shame worked. Turns out, shame is jet fuel for addiction. Cause of death? Write down shame. Sure as a bullet.

When the good people, the correct people, of Jackson County Georgia learned of my father's felony record, they hauled him in front of a judge and disbarred him. They stripped him of his license and the title of "city solicitor." He died alone in a hotel room about nine months later, the shame growing inside him, fueled by fifth after fifth of Smirnoff. I'd believe in shame if shame worked.

My father had set about to clean up his record, posting a legal ad in the Baton Rouge *Advocate*. But while you can fix guilt, you can't scrub shame. America may have once been the land of second chances, but not the land of the fourth or fifth chance. My father had run out of chances.

Why do I gravitate toward women? Not for sex. Not anymore. I've never once confused a therapist with a sex worker. Different magazines in the waiting room. Maybe I trust women's judgment more. Maybe I find them more empathic. Maybe I'm still just a little boy who misses his mommy.

I've been to see Tammy off and on over the course of fourteen years. I once expressed my gratitude and admiration by putting her up for a community service award. They gave it to her at a big banquet at the Westin Charlotte. "One of my clients is in big trouble," she told the crowd as the waiters poured coffee. I gave her a rare hug after. I said, "The words you're looking for are 'thank you.'"

I'll listen to Tammy. I give great weight to her insight. I'll let her words land, not feel the need to react. She has the most finely calibrated bullshit detector of anyone I've ever met.

One session I was going on and on about how my life never amounted to anything. She interrupted with two distinct words, "Bull. Shit." She proceeded to recite my resumé and sum up by pronouncing me a decent husband, dad, and friend. "If that's all you ever amount to," she said, "I guess you're just gonna have to live with it." I had no comeback.

The primary way I am wrong is in thinking I'm bad. I'm not ashamed of my sin. The shame *IS* the sin. Let go of shame. Own where I'm wrong. Acknowledge guilt, and the sin of shame falls away.

I'd believe in shame if shame worked. I don't earn redemption. I accept forgiveness.

"I'm not ashamed of my sin. The shame IS the sin. Own where I'm wrong. Acknowledge guilt, and the sin of shame falls away."

. . . .

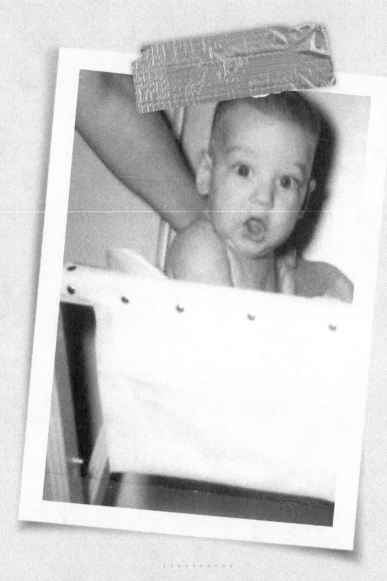

Me. Albany, Georgia. 1960.

FREEDOM

. . . .

"You're free."

Therapist name withheld by request.
Charlotte, North Carolina
2018

On Letting Go

HER: There is nothing standing between you and what you really want and really need to contribute in this life. So what is it that you want?

ME: I'm terrified to say what I want.

HER: Why is that?

ME: Because it feels selfish and narcissistic to be so demanding. To talk about my needs first.

HER: Where did you get that idea?

ME: From my parents, I guess. I was told I was a spoiled, selfish child.

HER: Who spoiled you?

ME: Hm.

HER: Once they're off the hook, you're free.

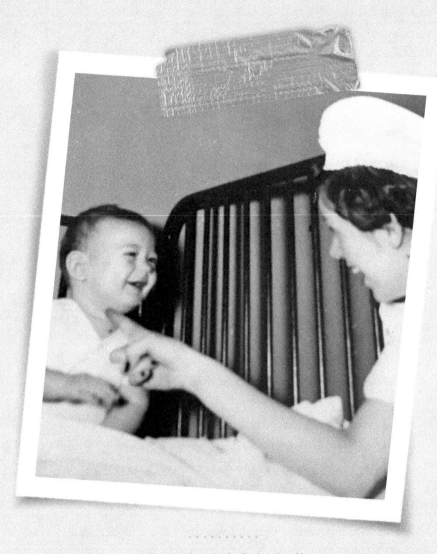

Little boy with Natalie Scully, RN. Brooklyn,
New York. Late 1940's.

THE LITTLE BOY, ALWAYS

. . . .

"There's not enough love in the world."

Natalie, my wife's mom
Near Syracuse, New York
2019

On Compassion

When one son came out as gay, his mother already knew. She had known since he was a little boy, but when he said it out loud to her and to her husband, I'm told she had but one reaction. "There's not enough love in the world."

I took it as her way of saying, "I love you." I see her say wordlessly to each of her six children: "I have always loved you, and I will always love you, and that means I affirm you because of who you are."

But with this son declaring his identity to them, it was her way of saying, "I understand." It was her way of asking a question, "Who am I, who is anyone, to say you're not OK, when you are adding love by leaps and bounds to a world so often deprived of it?"

My wife's brother has been with his partner longer than Lorraine and I have been married. They never married. Now they're retiring together.

When I first met Natalie, I was a young hunk with a beard, forty years and forty pounds ago, dating her daughter. I drank their beer, raiding the fridge all day, and then I drank their wine with the elaborate dinners Natalie prepared. Then I turned to their crystal decanters to drink their liquor all night.

Each day, Natalie threw enough food in the oven to last most families a week—a whole turkey, a whole pork roast, a whole leg of lamb. She didn't seem to believe in leftovers. I ate it all. But I focused on drinking.

We were down at the beach, must have been Sanibel Beach Club II, a timeshare ownership condo. We'd all gone out to dinner that night at the Timbers on Rabbit Road. My mom had followed us down on spring break to snoop. She held out the pretense of chaperoning my sister and her friend on neighboring Captiva, to South Seas Island Resort. I think Mom was really just curious about this new girl I was dating, this non-WASP Yankee, and about her people. Was this going to be a new daughter?

Mom told me to pick up the tab, but I was too drunk to pick up anything, and besides Lorraine's father, Dr. Jivoff, never let anyone pay the bill. Leo Jivoff was a son of New York City, the only child of Russian immigrants by way of Ellis Island. The US Army took one look at his medical aptitude scores and diverted Doc from a unit bound for the Battle of the Bulge, sending him instead to Princeton. I fell in love with him and Natalie—almost as much as Lorraine. If she ever wises up and divorces my ass, I demand custody of the in-laws—all of them.

That particular night on Sanibel Island, I was pounding one of those froufrou island drinks, and I know my head was sagging. At one point, I actually rested my forehead on the dinner table right in the middle of the restaurant. I was sitting at one head of the long table with Lorraine and some friends. Doc sat at the other end, he and Natalie charming my mom.

I went back to the condo with my future in-laws. They were driving, thank God. I was in no shape. They started watching *The Wizard of Oz* on the TV in the living room. I was tired. I'd had a lot of sun and a lot of liquor. I passed out cold at the foot of the bed. Lorraine's parents' bed. In the master bedroom. Pretty soon, the Master came in and wanted to use his own bed. He shook me. I may have stirred, but I didn't budge. That's when Natalie said, "Leave the boy alone, Leo. He's had a lot to drink."

It was the way she said the word "lot" as in "a lot to drink" that said everything. It said Irish, and of course Catholic, Brooklyn, and Nurse. It was her way of saying to her husband, "We've got no say over whether she keeps this one or throws him back, but you have reached an immovable object." It sounded to me like she was a nurse addressing a doctor, saying in so many words, "Look, I know you may think med school taught you to diagnose drunks, but I know from drunks. I can sniff 'em out at 500 yards."

She knew "a LOT to drink" from the neighborhood. From the church. From the parties. From the lineage of a Scully great-grandpa off the boat from Ireland to become first a barkeep, then NYPD. Because of course he did. It was written in her wiry blue veins, this knowledge.

When Lorraine and I got married, my bride's mother helped her daughter with the dress, not technically a wedding dress but a lovely gown fit for a garden wedding. Lorraine wore a crown of flowers in her hair. We still have the circle of ribbons. We toss the crown of dried blooms on our Christmas tree each year. They take on the smell of the conifer.

When her husband's heart failed him for the last time, one spring day on Sanibel, Natalie asked that I write up a little eulogy for Doc, whom I dearly loved, and try to read it aloud at his memorial without weeping. I did not succeed. I paused. I gutted it out. She looked up from the first row. After, she said, "You outdid yourself, fella," the Brooklyn accent pouring through.

Now she is stooped and shuffles slowly with a walker or a steadying hand; her hair is thin and white, and she is thin and white. In her nineties, she still cooks dinner, with the help of round-the-clock aides who occupy the adjacent couch like family. We all eat like royalty—pork loin from Wegmans grocery, fresh corn on the cob, and heirloom tomatoes from roadside farmstands in upstate New York, as well as homemade chocolate-chocolate cake.

Somehow at dinner, I begin talking about a kid in my extended family. His mother spotted track marks on his arm. She is beside herself with worry he will OD and die on the streets. I talk not out of gossip but because this is family and we can speak of such things. My wife's sisters look down and fall silent. My wife's mom is usually quiet for dinner chat of topics foreign to her—things like "podcasts" or "user interface." Now she speaks, her words carrying more weight because of their economy. "So sad," she says. "Just always remember the little boy."

"
Leave the boy alone, Leo.
He's had a lot to drink."

. . . .

Lorraine Jivoff and Stuart Watson.
Wedding reception. Mint Museum
Randolph. Charlotte, North Carolina.

MAKING MARRIAGE WORK

. . . .

"We'll do it."

Lorraine Jivoff, my wife
University City
Charlotte, North Carolina
2019

On Respect

"WHY ARE YOU YELLING?" my wife yells back at me.
This is our thing. Our shtick. Our own comedic patter. Only
it's not funny. I get LOUDER. "BECAUSE YOU'RE NOT
LISTENING!" I don't feel heard. She doesn't feel heard. We're
stuck in a yelling loop.

"I've never told you to fuck off," I said recently.

"You've never used those words," she said.

Accurate.

So we spent $265 a session once every month or so for a couple
of years to get help. To break free of the same old loop. The back
and forth. And it helped. It's cheaper by the hour than divorce
attorneys. And totally worth it for a couple of empty nesters
determined not to become mere screaming housemates.

So what does $5,000 or so buy you in the way of couples coaching? Well, here's one jewel: the one way my partner most wishes to be loved is the single way it's most difficult for me to provide. And of course, the one way I wish to be loved is the single most difficult way for her.

I'm the one who bought Gary Chapman's *The 5 Love Languages* books. I read every page, underlined stuff, wrote in the margins, took the quiz in ink. She answered a few questions out loud under extreme duress. I'll cut to the chase.

She loves for us to work on projects together—like moving a heavy piece of furniture upstairs. It's a combination of acts of service and quality time. Given her choice, I think she'd choose quality time mostly, but she wanted that armoire moved. And it was easier moving that hernia buster than it was to move her.

Couldn't I just pay some real men hundreds of dollars to come and tote the one piece of furniture? Nope. That's dumb. "We'll do it," she said. I didn't like the sound of that word, "we."

I made one condition. I drove my fat ass up the street to the U-Haul and rented a heavy-duty dolly for $11. Turns out there's this invention. It's called the wheel. Round thing. Hunh. Came with no instructions.

With bulging veins, red faces, f-bombs as noun, verb, and gerund, we took that gut-busting hunk of wood up two landings and a big turn, gouging a deep groove in the drywall but leaving the stair rail intact.

I've never seen her prouder. She took pics of that stupid armoire in its new location and sent them to the kids in the family group chat. I'm thinking of making it my avatar photo. I do love this woman, and I take great joy in making her proud. This is a rare and beautiful thing. I move furniture once every millennium. Get back to me in the year 3000. For the next owner of our home: the armoire comes with the house. This is non-negotiable.

Now here's my way of most feeling loved. Nope, not sex. I'm sixty; things change. It's words. The love-languages guy calls them "words of affirmation." I'd simply call it encouragement. A compliment. She doesn't even have to mean it. But it takes five "attaboys" to offset one "aw shit." This is just science.

That's why her bragging to the kids about "your father moving furniture" means more to me than sex, Panthers tickets, or even her made-from-scratch veggie and goat cheese pizza. It means the converse is also true. The way I hurt her most is by hanging away from her with my friends, especially if those friends are younger and female. And it means the way she hurts me most is not just by withholding compliments, but by tossing sharp words like ninja stars.

In tandem, this abandonment/insult loop leads to the YELLING about NOT YELLING where we started. It doesn't matter which comes first, my days outside our home working with women or her running critique of my work. This isn't about blame. I can't own her stuff. After forty years together, I suffer few illusions that I can say the magic words at any volume to fundamentally change her. And I don't want to.

Her insistence on spending as much time together as possible is the whole reason I committed my life to this person. My sociability and involvement in the world, my comfort around connecting with people, must have attracted her at some level. And she doesn't want to deny me that. So I'm cautious about excising the fundamental attribute I most admire simply because I don't like the way it's being used. I perceive that she's "against me." She's just being herself. She's demanding what she needs. Would it really kill me to give it to her?

Here's how I shift. I cancel some plans. I blow off going to the baby shower for a young, female friend and instead spend time at home with Lorraine. We sit on the couch and watch an old movie. We read books side by side—her always fiction, me always non. Once in a great while, I move a piece of furniture. And oh yeah, I gotta lower my voice. I can get loud.

"

I hurt her most by hanging away from her. She hurts me most by hurling words like ninja stars."

. . . .

My sister, Esther Schmid Bristow.
Emanuel County, Georgia. Summer 2007.

ABANDONERS ABANDON

. . . .

"How do you know? You weren't even there."

Esther Bristow, my biological sister
Emanuel County, Georgia
2018

On Abandonment

My sister left me a chipper happy birthday voicemail, "I luv yooouuu, my brother," and died the next week. The elected coroner, who went to high school with Esther, put her cause of death as "multiple organ failure." I would have paid for an autopsy, but I'm a snoopy reporter who sticks his nose into other people's business. And it wasn't up to me.

I got the call from her middle child, Clay, a chiseled, likable salesman with a million dollar smile, living with a girlfriend in Miami. "Uncle Stuart, this will change your life. Mama is dead."

I first met my full-blood sister at one of Ted Turner's bison restaurants outside Atlanta. We were in our forties. Our brother Andy was with her. He and I went to a Braves game that night to get to know each other. At our first meeting, my long-lost brother told me, "It sucks growing up without a dad."

He said aloud what she felt. And how Esther reacted to
that great loss was eating. And eating. She kept eating because
something kept eating her. For the next fourteen or so years, when
Esther and I met, we ate. Food bonded us. We both obsessed over
food, whether we were eating or not eating.

Esther was a pretty blonde with a bright smile and a quick
laugh. She felt called to be a career nurse, even though our mother
was a lifelong nurse and strongly advised against it. Given that our
parents met at the notorious state mental hospital in Milledgeville,
my sister felt particularly drawn to mental health nursing,
especially among older patients. She hated how the system turned
its back on the most fragile among us. She called such brutal
apathy "I-don't-care land."

Esther had three children by three marriages, two sons and a
daughter. She went away to treatment centers more than once.
She loved the Lord and went with her husband, Tommy, to the
Hawhammock Baptist Church near Canoochee Creek, Georgia.
She loved her kids more than life itself. She lost custody of Clay
after a bad relapse. As we say in the South, it like to have killed
her. The judge recessed court for mere minutes, telling her, "Say
goodbye to your son."

She doted on her daughter so much that once after a relapse
and a single-car wreck, she checked herself out of the hospital
against medical advice saying, "I gotta get home to Bailey." It's just
a fact that Bailey totaled a car herself as a teenager, walked away,
and went on to have her own scrapes with the law. The loss of
Esther decimated her.

Esther became a grandmother by her eldest, Nick, who was
stationed in Japan with the Air Force. She worried about him

incessantly. She only quit smoking when he said she wouldn't be able to hold her grandson until she put away the cigarettes for good. She still vaped alongside her daughter Bailey.

When Esther married Tommy, it stuck. They met in recovery. They were both Baptists. They went on church mission trips together, bringing Bailey along. Tommy drove the church bus. He'd get mad and fly off the handle, and she'd eventually calm him down. He worked like a dog, up well before dawn, commuting hours each way first as a lineman and then as a safety supervisor at Georgia Power. Esther supported his part-time passion of cooking barbecue. Tommy had his own big grill welded together and put on wheels to tow behind the truck to weekend competitions.

Esther got along famously with Tommy's ex-wife, the mother of his first three children. They went on combined family vacations, rented houses together, brought the new spouses, and threw all the kids together. There was no such thing as a half-sibling or a step-anything. It was all just family. Esther called her husband's ex "my wife-in-law."

Esther had gastric bypass surgery in her thirties. She was forced on the scales when she was pregnant with Bailey, her youngest. She told me she came in at 325. When I met her, she had lost close to 200 pounds.

For addiction, like obesity, you've basically got three likely suspects. It's the old nature/nurture/free will multiple choice. You can blame DNA. You can blame trauma. And you can blame yourself. Or you can just say it was some combination without ever assigning blame. Me, I demand percentages. And it drove me crazy.

Esther arrived at 70/20/10—70 percent the sins of the father (and mother) by way of DNA, 20 percent the wounds of that

absent father (again what happened to us), and 10 percent
our own doing, a strange tithe of accountability. I've heard
different numbers batted about. From 50 percent to high 90s for
heritability. Some go to extremes, assigning zeros and a 100, taking
full responsibility or none at all. Free will versus determinism.

Esther knew we could be selfish. Our father could be
completely self-absorbed, and we are his kids, after all. Three of
us have the same mother, same father—Esther, Andy, and me.
Although I was put up for adoption and raised by parents who
rarely drank, all three of us grew up to develop "substance use
disorder." And all of us abused two primary substances to start:
food and alcohol. In Esther's case, complications from the first
addiction ended her life at fifty-seven. Our father died of acute
alcoholism at forty-six. Andy is now fifty-six, and as I type this, I'm
due to turn sixty-one tomorrow. While I'm in pretty good health,
it's no guarantee.

Esther's first substance of abuse did the most long-lasting
damage, the white powders. Not cocaine. Not China white,
the opioid. No, I'm talking about the three more deadly drugs
of abuse: sugar, white flour, and to a lesser extent, salt. Before
cigarettes, before vodka, before opioids or benzodiazepines, there
was the numbing comfort of biscuits and pancakes and donuts and
cookies and sugary cereal and chocolate and plain old mainline
solid sugar candy.

"Comfort comes as a guest, lingers to become the host,
and stays to enslave us," according to Hindu spiritual leader
Swami Chinmayananda.

I'm right there with her. My sister and I were both programmed
with the same code, the same X's and Y. I'll ride a sugary rush to

its glycemic spike and inevitable crash, nodding out like a junkie. And nodding is just the beginning. It's the lifetime of extra strain on the gut that gets you. Multiple organ failure. Our organs fail us because we failed them.

Why can some people have one bite and walk away while others throw food down their gullets as maniacal as dope fiends? I don't know about everyone, but in our case, I find our absent father guilty on two out of three counts: genes and trauma.

After one of Esther's relapses, I stopped by the house she, Tommy, and their daughter Bailey shared with our mother, three strong-willed generations under one roof. Our mother had deeded the house to my sister with the understanding that Esther would care for our mother in her old age. I sat on a sofa across the wide room and began to preach to Esther about getting back to meetings, to the recovery community. When she'd offer a lame excuse, I countered with, "That sounds like something our father would have said."

I touched a raw nerve, our father's abandonment.

"How do you know?" she snapped. "You weren't even there."

That's when our mother spoke up, leaning back in her easy chair: "Don't you remember honey? Just before he left, he said, 'Even you don't love me.'"

Let's get this straight. A forty-six-year old father walks out on his eight-year-old daughter, and among the last words he speaks to her before drinking himself to death are, "Even you don't love me."

Wow. That'll leave a mark. How—please tell me—how is an eight-year-old girl supposed to fill such a bottomless pit of neediness and self-pity? She couldn't. So she just kept eating until finally her gut would no longer process the pain, and she starved, dehydrated, her blonde hair brittle and her pallor gray.

When she went to therapy, she told me they kept coming back to the absent father who left when she was eight. She said she'd like to have a sit-down with that guy. Sort some things out. Maybe now she has.

WATCH, LISTEN, AND LEARN

To hear Esther tell her story, visit ManListening.com or wherever you get your podcasts to hear the full podcast episode titled "Esther Bristow."

"

For addiction, like obesity, you've basically got three likely suspects. It's the old nature/ nurture/free will multiple choice. You can blame DNA. You can blame trauma. And you can blame yourself."

. . . .

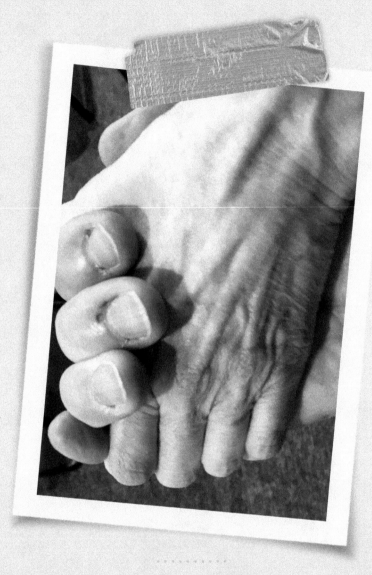

Holding hands with my friend Gay.
Dilworth Center. Charlotte, North Carolina.
February 2020.

JAMIE HAS GONE TO HEAVEN

. . . .

"A miracle is a change of perception."

Gay, my friend
C3 Lab
Historic South End
Charlotte, North Carolina
2019

On Miracles

"Watch Jamie," her mother instructed as she went away to get the baby changed for church. My friend Gay was six years old, only a few years older than her brother Jamie, who was little more than a toddler. She did not watch Jamie. Instead, Gay and her sister ran into the backyard to play under the grey moss. Jamie toddled into the pond in front of the house. She never saw him again.

When people would ask Gay about the impact of Jamie's death on her parents, she'd say, "It's OK. They had more boys." But what about the impact on her? No one asked. They just didn't talk about it. Her parents sat the kids down once and explained, "Jamie has gone to heaven." After that they didn't speak of it. They bypassed the drowning part. For a while, Gay was afraid to take baths.

It wasn't until she was in her twenties, with a lot of anxiety and a lot of drinking, that Gay went to see a therapist. The therapist heard the story of Jamie and gently explained to Gay that this was a big deal. It was unresolved.

Decades into twelve-step recovery I learned several basics about addiction that surprised me:

1. Trauma is quite prevalent in the adolescence of the addict.
2. We addicts can numb the pain but never heal it as long as we use.
3. My trauma is not your trauma; these wounds take many forms.

In my twelve-step group alone, I know of two other people who witnessed the death of a baby brother, both by falling. One fell out a window and survived, then fell off a bed and did not. The other boy's death was in New York City. The big brothers were swinging the child by his arms and legs in front of an open window and in a moment just let go.

And fatal accidents are just one kind of trauma. I haven't touched the mountains of molestation, shootings, and stabbings, not to mention mothers and fathers, often addicted themselves, who abandoned future addicts in innumerable ways.

"Millennials have had it so easy," another boomer told me. "What do they have to complain about?" This particular boomer's son flatlined on heroin, his heart stopping before the medics hit him with naloxone and brought him back. Tests found cocaine and meth in his system as well. He went right back out there. I'm trying to talk to my fellow boomer about trauma, how for the children of 9/11, it doesn't all look the same.

Until I was fifty-six years old, I didn't think I was allowed to have trauma. My friend Tommy taught me different. He'd been shot multiple times and hit with shrapnel in Iraq. Before I ever even met him face-to-face, I was explaining to him on the phone how he got to have trauma, but I didn't. He was an American Hero. I'd been a drunken frat boy. I was comparing. He cut me off: "It's not a dick-measuring contest."

Everyone's wounds are different. It's not a competition. We're not in the trauma Olympics. Me? I thought if you've got rape, torture, or war in your story, you're allowed. You're in the club. If you were cut from your mother and stuck in foster care as an infant, suck it up. You had a good life. You should be grateful. Don't go blaming your troubles on others. I hadn't read Bessel van der Kolk's *The Body Keeps the Score* and understood what got hardwired into my nervous system when I was taken from my mother.

Yes, comparison is the thief of joy, as Teddy Roosevelt said, but it's also the stumbling block to resilience. We each have our own wounds. I can't ever really bounce back with a gaping wound unattended. It's basic mental health triage. First, we stem the bleeding, stop tearing it open again and again. Then we create a safe environment free of unhealthy infection. Then we close the wound. Finally, we begin to heal.

Gay lost her brother, then her marriage, and then her son to a heroin overdose. If she wanted to swill wine and eat pills all day, I'd completely understand. But she doesn't. She is a vital part of a vibrant community of recovery. I hear her on the regular refer to the benevolence of the universe that is nothing short of an Old Testament miracle.

How in the world? Where was this benevolence when her brother drowned, and her marriage fell apart, and her son overdosed? I asked her to sit down and record a conversation with me, to explain how she got from completely broken to healed to resilient.

She said a miracle is a change of perception. No amount of thinking would change her personal tragedies. But she believed she could petition the universe and sit in silence, and she began to perceive the same facts in a completely new way. Answers would come. And for her, they did. In her case, she used a specific type of meditation called "centering prayer." She used a Sanskrit word, not as a mantra but as a call to her brain to return from a thousand crazy thoughts to one universal truth, a truth bigger than life and death. And she found peace. She will always grieve, but she's found respite, a place of calm.

Jamie's death was not Gay's fault, not her mother's fault, not her sister's. My wounds are not the same as Gay's, neither greater nor less. We are each clean and free through the miracle of healing called recovery. Resilience takes longer. It's not a race.

WATCH, LISTEN, AND LEARN

To hear Gay tell her own story, visit ManListening.com and stream the full episode, "Gay B."

"

Everyone's wounds are different.
It's not a competition. We're
not in the trauma Olympics."

· · · · · · · · · · · · ·

Me and Colleen after the Midsouth
Regional Emmys. Winter 2014.
Nashville, Tennessee.

AN UNANSWERED QUESTION

. . . .

"Why did they fire you?"

Fabi Preslar
Publisher
SPARK Publications
March, 2020

On Honesty

Sometimes former colleagues will say to me, "When you left the TV station…"

I cut them off. "I didn't leave. They fired me."

They'll say, "Oh. I was just trying to be nice."

"Don't be nice," I say. Be direct. It's not rude to avoid niceties and just be honest. Words matter. Getting laid off and getting fired are two totally different things. If I'd been laid off, I never would have written this. I'd be at some other TV station, warning you of rain or snow or slime in the ice machine.

So I appreciated it when Fabi didn't make any assumptions, just asked the question directly, "Why did they fire you?" She'd make a great investigative journalist, that Fabi.

Truth be told, I don't know why they fired me and I probably never will. I sued them for age discrimination and we settled for an undisclosed amount that I can't talk about. But it's not just that I can't say why I was fired. I don't even know. No one ever gave me a reason. But I'll give you my take. I've spent more than five years wrestling with this. I've written and rewritten this chapter many times. The answers I come up with run along three story lines:

1. They were assholes.
2. I was the asshole.
3. It had to happen, and thank God it did.

I can write whole volumes on story #1, my victim story. That's a story you tell a bartender, and I don't do that anymore. So I'm gonna spare you.

I think story #2 is equally tedious, the endless self-flagellating. It also ends at the liquor store, a place I can ill afford.

The just-business answer I gave Fabi had to do with a corporate buyout and the need to cut costs. Now as the beast eats its own tail, the ones who sacked me have themselves been sacked.

So the only story worth telling is #3. Getting fired absolutely had to happen. And it had to happen in exactly the way it did. This is sometimes called fate, or synchronicity, or God's will, or dumb luck, depending on your spiritual disposition or lack thereof.

Here's what I mean. I reset the chessboard and played out all the various moves in this sequence, and getting fired (not "laid off" or "let go") is the best possible thing that could have happened.

Let's say the new bosses kept me on after the big merger. I would have been abjectly miserable seeing what happened to the newsroom that I poured my heart and soul into. That scenario would have been the absolute worst thing—keeping my job and going down with the ship.

Let's say they gave me six month's notice and encouraged me to find work elsewhere. I would have sulked and been resentful. Not the worst case, but not good either. I'd have taken my bad attitude to the next newsroom only to anxiously await being fired there.

Let's say they gave me a recommendation and moved me elsewhere in the company, a promotion. A little better for my ego maybe. But I have deep roots in North Carolina, lots of sources and contacts, plus all my kids went to UNC schools and three out of four live here. So I would not have wanted to relocate.

Let's say they encouraged me to find work in a different profession, like teaching. I'd make a great teacher, a life-changing professor; I love learning from and with bright minds, and I respect millennials and Gen Zers. But in practical terms, I don't have a master's degree. UNC and others wouldn't even look at me without a master's. That would mean starting over by going back to school for a new profession that wasn't my idea. I thought about it. Didn't make sense.

Now look at what DID happen.

I spent five years soul searching, listening instead of talking, in a self-imposed exile of sorts, a prolonged sabbatical. I wandered in this wilderness. I kept asking myself what I really want to contribute in the last twenty years or so of my life. Is my obituary really already written? I don't think so. When Théoden Janes interviewed me for the *Charlotte Observer*, he paid me one of the greatest compliments any journalist could.

He said, "It could be in the end that you are not remembered for Emmys or Peabodys, or local TV news at all, but for whatever you do now." Wow! Somebody was listening.

I didn't sit around and mope for that five years. Quite the contrary. I flew around the country shooting interviews for a documentary, all of which I still have. That means I have interviews with people like my sister Esther and my mother's brother "Big L." Both have since died. If I had kept my little TV job, I would have missed my one chance to record those warm, rich voices. I never would have gotten the time off to do it right.

If I had waited just a few years before speaking to my mother on camera, her memory and command of language would not have been nearly so sharp, let alone her ability to travel with me to places like the ruins of the mental hospital at Milledgeville. There, we walked around and reminisced on camera and she told me how she met my father. Now she does not walk or drive. That thread of Georgia's oral history, so incredibly meaningful to me, would have been lost forever. As it is, I've preserved it. I can return to it after this book is put to bed.

I created the podcast ManListening®, wrote this book, and I have my speaking or teaching or coaching, plus other creative projects yet to be revealed.

Had I made a plan and forced the issue, I would be ending a career in much the same way I started, having learned very little about myself. Why did they fire me? Because they had to. Otherwise I wouldn't be doing what I was meant to. Mysterious ways. Wondrous to behold.

"

*It could be in the end that you are
not remembered for Emmys or
Peabodys or local TV news at all,
but for whatever you do now.*"

— *Théoden Janes*

. . . .

Jack's first shave. University City.
Charlotte, North Carolina. 2010.

TURTLE SHOVED JACK IN THE RIVER

· · · · · · · · · · · · · · · ·

I don't remember what she said, but she was livid.

Lorraine Jivoff, my son's mom
New River, West Virginia
2020 (from an incident in 2006)

On Redemption

Our stair rail wobbled at the first landing. Turtle came over and fixed it. Funny. I never thought of him as a stabilizing force. He wouldn't take money for the job. He wanted to sit down at the family dinner table and join in. Lorraine made her typical hot meal from scratch, which we all took for granted. All except our guest.

He had drunk his way out of his own family—the drinking and the bipolar—and signed away all parental rights to his two girls. I don't think he was ever really able to forgive himself. More than a hot meal, I think he took comfort in a family.

His ex-wife called me once at the TV station to complain how horrible he was to her and their girls. Said that I should investigate him, expose him on the news. I never told her I knew him. I never told anyone that she called. Not until now.

The name Turtle came from his time as a whitewater guide on the New and Gauley rivers up in West Virginia. Seems when you flip one of those rafts upside down, it looks like a turtle shell. It was their way of saying he flipped a lot of boats. The name stuck among some of us. His friend Bruce read the lyrics to the Grateful Dead's "Terrapin Station" at his funeral.

I took Lorraine and our kids and our westie Clarence up I-77 to West Virginia one weekend when the kids were small. Turtle offered us a raft trip through some of the smaller rapids. He wouldn't take money for that either. Just wanted a meal with us.

We had to park our minivan down by the New River, near the famous span bridge at the end of our route. Then we all piled in his small truck with the big raft covering the bed, and he drove the bumpy switchbacks to put in upriver. We men sat up in the front seat. Turtle smoked cigarettes, windows open. We put Lorraine and the kids and the dog in the truck bed under the raft. A thunderstorm struck before we could put in. Lorraine tried to reassure the kids sheltering under the raft. It didn't stop us.

Turtle never had a son. He liked to give my son Jack a hard time. Jack must have been around eight back then. On the flat water after one of the rapids, Turtle shoved Jack out of the raft. He thought it was funny. Lorraine was livid. Jack was terrified. I kinda laughed it off. I was caught between my wife and my buddy, between female and male, my son in the middle. I felt deep shame. I felt like I took sides with a bully against my own son.

Turtle fished a screaming, sputtering Jack out of the New River by his life vest. I think Turtle felt bad about it. He encouraged Jack to push him in the river to make things even. He got his cigarettes all wet. He made an effort. No one ever forgot it. My son had long since left home for college, and Turtle would still ask me, "How's Jack?"

Turtle got fired from that whitewater job. I think more than one of them. He smack-talked a woman, I heard. I lost touch with him, didn't see him around the rooms of recovery much anymore. He got remarried, an adventure in itself. He'd get depressed and hole up alone.

Then one morning, I heard Turtle hung himself. The story was he called 9-1-1 and then did it. They kept him breathing for three or four days on a vent while they located his sisters. Our friend Bruce went to the hospital. He watched Turtle. And I believe Turtle watches him, still.

It was cold and raining the night of the funeral. But I'm not sure if you would have gotten better attendance on a warm spring morning. A lot of us who did show up spoke. The minister had to cut it off. Then they had a reception for his daughters and his sisters to hear more stories, a different side of this stranger, this kin. No brother, no father, no son was there. I heard his brother had also taken his life the year before.

Here is the story I told at the funeral, more or less: "I was tricked into taking my family on one of Turtle's raft trips. None of us will ever forget it. Turtle shoved my son, Jack, out of the boat. My wife is still mad about it." (The women in his family seemed to nod. Sounded about right.)

"I called up Turtle last year because I wanted to understand something he told me about the whitewater. I wanted to use it in some story I was writing. He said there was a particular pothole on the New River where you could easily drown. The rapids would push you down, down, down to the bottom. He said the mistake people make is in fighting. Like a riptide at the beach, the trick is to stop fighting and go with the powerful flow down, down, all the way down to the bottom. Then, and only then, will this force of nature shoot you skyward. Turtle went down, down, all the way down to the bottom. Now he is shooting up to the light."

(I looked his daughters, these strangers, in the eye.)

"Never doubt this."

"

Like a riptide at the beach, the trick is to stop fighting and go with the powerful flow ..."

. . . .

Zuzu the westie, me, and Lorraine.
Christmas tree shopping. Near Boone,
North Carolina.

A PRETTY COOL COUPLE

. . . .

"I'm very proud of you."

Lorraine Jivoff (we hooked up)
University City
Charlotte, NC
February 14, 2020

On Affirmation

I didn't get Lorraine a Valentine card this year. She says she didn't miss it. I'm not sure I believe that. She got me one. It had a pink, white, and blue popsicle with two sticks and two smiley faces and on it was printed, "We're a pretty cool couple." In it she wrote:

I'm glad to be on this journey with you. I love you and if I don't say it often enough — I'm very proud of you! xoxo Lorraine

In lieu of a card, I took her on a couple of overnight trips at opposite ends of North Carolina. We drove over to Asheville and walked around the art galleries down by the river. I bought a book at Malaprop's, and we had breakfast with dear friends as their guests at The Inn on Biltmore Estate. Then we drove over to the Western North Carolina Nature Center and saw the otters get fed and stopped by Looking Glass Creamery for cheese before driving back past Chimney Rock and Lake Lure.

The next weekend I got asked to speak at a twelve-step meeting in Kinston, 250 miles east. We made a night of it with a late dinner reservation at the Chef & the Farmer, the place run by Vivian Howard on PBS. Lorraine had her usual manhattan, up, with Basil Hayden's top-shelf bourbon. I had tonic water. We both had wonderful meals.

I booked a little garden cottage on Airbnb in New Bern, a cozy place owned by a woman who works as an airline pilot. Lorraine and I walked by the Neuse River on a blustery morning, white caps on the water. We stopped on the way back to Charlotte and picked up our westie Zuzu from our youngest daughter, who agreed to dog sit. We took Colleen out to lunch at a Mediterranean deli, Neomonde, in downtown Durham. Zuzu waited impatiently back in Colleen's bedroom, sniffing the cats, Neko and Katie, under the door.

We each give the other the thing it is hardest to give. She gives me words of affirmation. I give her quality time in our one precious life together.

"

We each give the other the thing it is hardest to give."

. . . .

Administering wedding vows to Amy
Correll in her marriage to Tim McDonnell.
Lake Norman. Mooresville, North
Carolina. May 30, 2020. Photo courtesy
of Tate Finley.

BREATH

. . . .

"I will... I do."

Amy Correll
Bride
Lake Norman
Mooresville, NC
May 30, 2020

On Abundance

In the weird time-out-of-time that was the COVID-19 quarantine, May 2020 started for me with a funeral and ended with a wedding. I attended the first ritual and performed the second, both in person, a calculated risk. In these times any human connection was a calculated risk, be it handshake, hug, or unmasked belly laugh.

Farewell to the Judge

My dear friend Nancy Stephenson died on April 1. Her funeral was on May 1. In between, the family had no human contact, only an intimate Zoom call to share memories. (As intimate as a webcam can be, that is.) There they looked into pixels, not eyes. It's just not the same.

Her husband John was stuck in the house where she died, alone. They wheeled her out around midnight. The neighbors saw the ambulance pull up and gathered at the curb, watching from a distance, and praying.

I called him as soon as I heard. "She was the air I breathe," he said. He wasn't breathing well either. I offered to drive the six hours down, just to stand outside his window. "Please don't," he said. "It's not safe." Albany, Georgia had made the *New York Times* as an epicenter of the COVID outbreak.

Nancy was a probate judge in my hometown, married to one of my oldest friends. She'd been elected and reelected for twenty-seven continuous years. John's a judge as well. She always reminded him she was the senior judge. She could pull rank. Together they were known as "The Judges Stephenson."

It's hard to capture how sweet and kind and quirky and funny Nancy was. The preacher told a story at her graveside service that gets close.

It was warming up by mid-morning at Riverside Cemetery, the one along the Flint River that flooded twice in the '90s with the caskets popping to the surface and floating away. Everyone wore face masks and spread out among the headstones in ones and twos. Only the family gathered under the shade of the tent. John predicted thirty people would attend. I counted three times that. There were judges and lawyers and deputies in uniform.

The story: it seems the Methodist preacher arrived in the hospital room just in time for another death in the Stephenson family, but this one was expected. The family had all gathered around the bed. The pastor was there to give comfort.

He stayed to bear witness to the last breath. It was a long, uncomfortable moment. No one said a word. Minutes passed. Nancy broke the silence. She turned to the pastor and said, "If I'm ever in a hospital bed and I see you coming, I'm going to get up and leave."

Nancy would have wanted the laughter. I can't tell you how much we needed laughter.

She didn't see it coming. None of us saw it coming. She left before we could say goodbye.

Then, the new magistrate, Victoria Johnson, stepped to the mic to sing "Amazing Grace." She replaced John when he moved up to judge. She's a deaconess at the Mount Zion Baptist Church and sung with the New Freedom Singers. The mic cut in and out. She didn't need it. Her voice carried across the cemetery, pure and clear as the bubbling blue water from the artesian springs in this city. That's when Judge Johnson gave us a great gift: the gift of grieving.

For a moment no one quibbled with the hymn writer's problematic history in the slave trade. The audience of Georgia Bulldogs was mainly relieved that Judge Johnson did not wear her Florida Gator mask. She considered her audience.

Nancy had a huge heart. She once confided in me her worries for a person she loved dearly who had been all wrapped up in his addiction. I shared what experience I could. No advice. She texted me back, "You're such a great friend. I'm glad you figured it out. Our life would be significantly poorer without you."

Nancy was a great friend. I'm not sure any of us ever really figures it out. My life is significantly richer because she was in it. But it's sadder without her.

What a Wonderful World

I'm pretty sure it was Amy's idea that I perform their wedding, but Tim went along with it. Nine months before the ceremony, they conceived the whole thing. They took me out to Showmars on East Boulevard and bought me a salad, the Greek one with the salmon on top, and popped the question: "Will you marry us?"

"Is this some kind of three-way?" I asked. "A thruple? What am I getting into?" JK. Of course I didn't say that.

I was mainly baffled. Why me? "We don't want any bullshit," Amy said. I totally love her endorsement of me as her go-to no-bullshit clergy. So I sent the Universal Life Church my email address and was ordained on the spot. I spent another thirty or forty bucks on certificates and a fuchsia short-sleeve shirt with a white clerical collar (which I have never worn in public). As I modeled my pretense of piety in the kitchen for my family, they responded as one: "Ugh."

Almost three months into the quarantine, we didn't know if there would be a wedding, as planned. Tim and Amy had plunked down good money on renting a gorgeous lakefront home up near the NC 150 bridge. With just weeks to spare, the governor lifted the ban on gatherings just enough to permit a couple of dozen well-spaced guests. It was on.

Tim and Amy had each married before and they had teenaged kids who got along like a house afire. That's a good thing. From early on, Amy's kids liked "Mr. Tim." Tim's kids liked "Mimi."

The whole thing felt very relaxed. It felt right. It was like a weekend house party on the lake with a wedding thrown in.

Tim plays bass in a couple of bands and owns his own painting contracting company. He's a creative guy and an entrepreneur. I really look up to him. Amy works in the recovery field at the Dilworth

Center. Without going into detail, let's just say they're both grateful to be alive, let alone finding love and each other.

I felt overwhelmingly privileged. I wanted to give them the wedding they dreamed of. I wasn't weighed down with a bunch of "thees" and "thous," or a millennia of theology like barnacles on a sunken ship. I took my lead from them.

Tim hired a former bandmate and his wife to play "What a Wonderful World." Our friend Dave got together a professional video crew to livestream the whole thing for anyone who couldn't make it. Between Facebook Live and Instagram Live, more than a thousand people bore witness. I can't tell you how much we needed human contact.

The kids escorted each other two-by-two down the hill to the lakeside. Tim wore his best porkpie hat. I wore a jacket and a white T-shirt with our friend Drew Harkey's smiling mug on it. (Drew died a couple of years ago. It's my way of inviting him to crash the party.) Amy wore the perfect dress. I can't describe it. I'm a man. It was pretty, OK? She said she paid $30 for it online. Her hair and makeup could easily have cost ten times that. It was all worth it. She was resplendent.

When the kids were riding jet skis the day before, one of the neighbors yelled at 'em. Called 'em white trash. Really? These Iredell County newcomers clearly need to get in their Range Rovers and drive around more. Whatever. The show went on. We got the couple hitched without a hitch.

Most of the guests knew each other, but we hadn't seen each other face-to-face in almost three months. It's hard to say how much human contact means, being together as a group. It's life-sustaining. Alone, we wither. Together, we flourish.

I'll spare you my sermon. Amy specifically wanted f-bombs, livestream be damned. I was there for the bride. I dropped 'em in the first sentence, just to set the tone. No one fainted. I took a moment of silence for everyone to invite their own Higher Power to be present. Then I took another moment of silence for everyone to invite whoever they wanted, on this side or the other, a great cloud of witnesses not subject to mortal law. Once welcomed, the spirits came, spilling up the hillside and under the trees, past the Adirondack chairs and back towards the lake house.

I read over the wedding vows several times before the ceremony, but I still tucked the paper in my jacket pocket to make sure I got them word for word. Amy had written the vows for Tim. Tim had written the questions for Amy. Three questions each. Easy peasy? Not really.

As I turned to Amy, she had tears in her eyes. Before the final question, my paper says, "PAUSE BEFORE SAYING." Suddenly it dawned on me. Each partner is asking of the other the hardest thing. Amy asked for what she needs that's hardest for Tim to give: the attention she deserves. Then Tim asked Amy for what he needs, it's the hardest for Amy to give: a vow not to run away, one day at a time.

Amy was crying. I started to lose it. I kept it together enough to pose the question. Do you promise not to abandon this man?

Amy responds, "I do."

None of us look back—only forward, the horizon rolling onward to new vistas, new days.

"
Alone we wither.
Together we flourish. **"**

. . . .

Lorraine as a bride. Cheekwood Estate &
Botanical Gardens. Nashville, Tennessee.
September 17, 1983. Photo courtesy of
Kats Smith Barry

EPILOGUE

. . . .

I found this note in my handwriting inside the cover of my copy of *Paths to Recovery*. I must have written it, but it doesn't sound like me. I think it came straight from the Muse herself.

"When threatened, respond from the voice of The Mother:

I know you.

I have recorded your whole history, every detail, in a place where it can never be erased.

You are preserved. You will live forever in my memory.

You are important. You matter.

You make a difference, far beyond your understanding.'"

When threatened, Respond from the voice of The Mother. I know you. I have recorded your whole history, even detail, in a place where it can never be erased. You are preserved. You will live forever in my memory. You are important. You matter. You made a difference far beyond your understanding.

The whole fam damily. Clockwise Colleen,
Erin, Jack, Glynis, me, Lorraine. Mint Street.
Charlotte, North Carolina. Photo courtesy
of Michael Harrison.

ACKNOWLEDGMENTS

· · · · · · · · · · · · · · ·

Lorraine Jivoff is and always will be the single most influential person in my whole life. She is a New York Yankee. I am a Georgia Cracker. She is a Taurus. I am an Aries. In the Enneagram I think she is a #1 perfectionist (although I'm not supposed to say that). I think I am a #2 giver. Yet here we are soulmates, each other's greatest teachers. To say I love her doesn't begin to describe it.

Erin Jivoff Watson, wordsmith, poet and zine creator, looked over my first offerings with a writerly eye. Up there in Chicago, she never looked down on me. She'd note "great" and "not great." Glynis Jivoff Watson shared her story with me, as much as she could bear. I'm sorry I was such a poor listener. She makes me want to get better. Colleen Jivoff Watson is writing her own book right now. Her diligence inspires me. Jack Jivoff Watson listened and listened and listened to me. Then he listened some more. One summer he listened for 5,500 miles in a meadering trip from Tucson to Seattle. It meant the world to me.

Nell Kerns Martin Watson once told me that whenever she heard talk of equal rights for women everywhere, a spark was ignited in her heart. Thus, she lit a fire in me. G. Stuart Watson loved and supported me even when he didn't understand me. He still does. His life's work makes my life's work possible. Liz Watson

Fort wishes we'd leaned on each other more as kids. It's never too late.

Helen Brett Schmid paid a heavy price to start a friendship with her firstborn so late in life. I'm forever grateful for her open heart. H. Scott Schmid endowed me with a nimble mind and a thimbleful of charm. That, and alcoholism. Esther Schmid Bristow spoke the language of the heart. We will see her again in the twinkling of an eye. Andy Schmidt helps me understand how important it is to have a father who sticks and stays. He stands by Sam and Eli.

Anne Heffron emailed me after our first "Write or Die" exercise. I was in tears. She was in tears. She said I'd be done with this book before the pavement was dry. Took years for that pavement to dry. But no way this book gets done without her.

Alix Felsing taught me how to round up my scattered thoughts like wild horses and put them in various pens to tame.

Tammy Bell encourages me not to abandon myself or anyone else, and so to break the cycle. Betty Hutcheson showed us a way to speak to each other and a way to listen. Pam Cordano coaches me to accept the abundance of the universe.

The Unnamed Therapist once threatened to turn me over to her lawyer if I misquoted her. Yikes! I am still grateful for her lessons.

Sally Higgins lawyered the final manuscript to try to keep me out of trouble. Fingers crossed.

The people who fired me saved my life. Without that, I would never have let go of local TV news. Or published this book. Or done the work that only I must do.

Leighton Grant, Dan Robbins, Rodney King, Terry Shiels, and Dave Stiles all shot great video so I can someday turn my story into a documentary film.

Al Bigley, Joel Kweskin and Callie Catchpole turned my zany ideas into art.

Kats Barry, Michael Harrison, Fred Clarke, Tate Finley, Michael LoBiondo, Emily Baxter, Mariano Archdeacon, Larry Patrick, and Rodney King all shot wonderful photographs.

Andrea Cooper, Libby Lucas, Diamond Nurse, Taylor Wright, Bernadette Joy, and Rob Monath help me develop, market, promote, and trademark the brand ManListening®. Allison Andrews, Rachel Clapp Miller, Roshanda E. Pratt, Catherine Smith, Brian Baltosiewich, and Meredith L. Carter help me develop, produce, and edit the podcast ManListening®.

Allison Andrews, Justin Faircloth, Tom Enright, and the Charlotte Mecklenburg Library's Morrison branch all loaned me quiet writing rooms for weeks at a time.

I need to acknowledge thousands of people in groups large and small who carried me for decades including: my **extensive family** of Bretts, Schmids, Watsons, Martins (McKinneys), and Jivoffs (Scullys); the **teachers, students, and staff** at Sherwood Elementary, Deerfield-Windsor School, Vanderbilt University, and Harvard University; **colleagues** at the *Albany Herald*, WRVU-FM, WSMV, WAPT, WTOL, WKRN, WRAL, WCNC, WBTV, WBT-AM, the *Charlotte Observer*, *Charlotte Magazine*, the Bob and Sheri Oddcast, Adoptees On, Author Accelerator, Investigative Reporters and Editors (IRE), the Poynter Institute for Media Studies, the Nieman Foundation for Journalism, the Society of Professional Journalists (SPJ), and Images & Voices of Hope (IVOH, now Peace Studio); **friends** at the First and Covenant Presbyterian Churches of Albany, GA, the Alpha Gamma Chapter of Zeta Beta Tau (ZBT), 202

Friendship House, Twelfth Step Service Inc., Anuvia, the Dilworth Center, the Back Room Group, the Gateway Meeting, Awakenings and New Awakenings Groups, Hair of The Dog, All Our Affairs (Leigh Ann), Springdale and Seneca groups, Chuck Maness CPA, Edmund Nobles at Regions Bank, Vic's Gym, Centre Medico Latino (Carlos & Nayla), Always Hungry Solution, Latakoo (Paul & Jade), Salon J Marco (Nikki Wilson), JC Signs, Park Road Books, Gratitude Training ML1 Charlotte, "Guinea Pigs" adoptees of Berkeley, CA, Veterans Bridge Home (Tommy and Dr. Nicole), "Atlantians" adoptees of Jersey City, NJ, Coming To The Table GA-Atlanta, Charlotte Center for Mindfulness, Enneagram Charlotte (Anne), A Course in Miracles (ACIM) at Unity of Charlotte, Interact Authentic Communication, OnQ Performing Arts, the Evening Muse, the Comedy Zone, the Queen City Podcast Network, C3 Lab, and Charlotte Lit; **the guys** on the 7:30 a.m. call every day, at breakfast on first Tuesdays all those years, on Zoom Sundays at 9 a.m., at Art's BBQ and Deli, Bedder Bedder & Moore, Community Matters Cafe, Park Road Soda Shoppe, and on Tim's back deck, and all my mentors and mentees trudging the road of happy destiny.

To **the supporters** who gave me more than $10,000 to make a documentary: I still owe you a film. First podcast, then book, THEN film, OK? I can't thank you enough!

Fabi Preslar, Shauna Sinyard, Jaclyn Miller, and Mel Graham at SPARK Publications gently find creative solutions to my word and image challenges. I use the "p-word." They write one word: "Nope." ;-)

Portrait by Michael LoBiondo

ABOUT THE AUTHOR

· · · · · · · · · · · · · · · · · ·

Stuart Watson created and trademarked ManListening® as a podcast and media company to start making amends for a lifetime of "mansplaining."

As an investigative reporter, Stuart is the three-time recipient of the coveted George Foster Peabody Award for excellence in broadcast journalism—at WKRN-TV (ABC) Nashville, TN, WRAL-TV (then CBS) Raleigh, NC, and WCNC-TV (NBC) Charlotte, NC.

He won the duPont-Columbia Silver Baton twice. He served three terms on the board of directors of Investigative Reporters and Editors (IRE) and was also awarded a Nieman Fellowship in Journalism at Harvard University.

Stuart was born in Macon and grew up in Albany, Georgia. He holds a Bachelor of Arts in English from Vanderbilt University (and they can't take it back).

Stuart, along with Lorraine Jivoff, coproduced Erin, Glynis, Colleen, and Jack. They call North Carolina home. #TARHEELS

MANLISTENING

· ·

Book Stuart Watson to speak
(or just listen)
at ManListening.com.

Contact him at
man@ManListening.com.

Talk back to him on most social
media @ManListening.